YOU, THE PARENT

by
Lawrence O. Richards

MOODY PRESS
CHICAGO

Contents

CHAPTER	PAGE

11213

Part 1
GUIDING PRINCIPLES

Now this is the commandment, the statutes and the judgments which the Lord your God has commanded me to teach you, that you might do them in the land where you are going over to possess it, so that you and your son and your grandson might fear the Lord your God, to keep all His statutes and His commandments, which I command you, all the days of your life, and that your days may be prolonged. O Israel, you should listen and be careful to do it, that it may be well with you and that you may multiply greatly, just as the Lord, the God of your fathers, has promised you, in a land flowing with milk and honey.

Hear, O Israel! The Lord is our God, the Lord is one! And you shall love the Lord your God with all your heart and with all your soul and with all your might. And these words, which I am commanding you today, shall be on your hearts; and you shall teach them diligently to your sons and shall talk of them when you sit in your house and when you walk by the way and when you lie down and when you rise up.

Deuteronomy 6:1-7

1
Life's Great Goal

You are a parent. In your home you can see
it: new personalities forming; new lives taking
shape. What will they be, these boys and
girls of yours? What do you want for them?
Here is where being a Christian parent begins;
with the realization that life has a goal and
that God has given you and me the exciting
privilege of taking our children by the
hand and leading them toward it!

God is Father. Probably we need to take our identity as parents from this truth. The Bible speaks of God as Father—Jesus' Father in a very special way, our Father because of Jesus.

Through looking at God as Father, you and I can best grasp what it means for us to be Christian parents. We can see in His love and His plan for us how we are to love and plan for our families. We can see in His relationship with us the relationships we are to build with our children. We can see in the ways He guides us the best practices for guiding our own children. It's true that the Bible does not often speak directly to parents saying, "Do this," or, "Don't do that." But the Bible does reveal the heart of our heavenly Father. And the Bible does reveal His gentle, yet firm, guiding hand.

This is what we are going to do together in this book. We are going to look at God our Father, explore what His Word reveals about Him and His rules for living with others, to see if somehow we can pattern ourselves as parents on Him.

This is really an important thing for us to study and explore. For God never presents Himself as "our heavenly Sunday school teacher." He does not tell us to communicate His life to our "class." God speaks of Himself as Father, and Scripture speaks ringingly to us as parents and charges us with the responsibility to bring up our *children* in the fear and admonition of the Lord.

I am not, of course, trying to criticize the many teachers who love the boys and girls they teach on Sunday mornings. But we do have to recognize the fact that it is the *home,* not the class, that shapes the life. The Bible states this truth and implies it in many ways. "Be imitators of God, as beloved children," Paul says to the Ephesians (5:1). Children may learn from their teachers, but they copy their parents. They become like their fathers.

Because of this, God says to parents in the Deuteronomy

passage around which these first three chapters are organized, "*You* shall teach them [God's words] diligently to *your* sons" (6:7, italics added). Being a Christian parent, molding new life toward God's goal, means far more than sending—or taking—our children to church. It means learning from God what it means to be a father. And learning from God how a parent communicates Christ, in a personality-shaping way, to his own children.

So it really is an important thing we're looking at in this book, something that I'm struggling to learn along with you. It is something that may become clearer—but not necessarily easier—as we go on together, looking to our heavenly Father to discover what it means for us to be Christian parents.

God has a goal

God's goal is something we can glimpse in the Old Testament. God is shown not only doing sweeping things—like creating, judging sin, and planning His coming kingdom. God is revealed to be deeply concerned about what is happening within individuals. God's work in our world has a personal focus.

Some have read the Old Testament superficially and summed up that focus as "obedience." God gave law. His people were to obey. Thus, what God wants from people— God's goal for us—is quick unquestioning obedience. Some Christian writers have picked up this idea and said to parents, "It's the goal of a parent to get his children to obey. To first obey him, and then learn to obey God."

There is truth in this idea, of course. But while there is truth, the understanding is superficial. And the notion that "our goal is to get our children to obey" is easily warped into something hateful and *un*true. For God's goal is *not* that we should obey Him. Obedience is instead a sign that God's real goal is being reached.

Deuteronomy 6. Moses spoke the words recorded in Deuteronomy 6:1-7 to God's people at a critical time in their history. They had been redeemed from Egypt, this generation and their parents. They had seen God's personal and miraculous intervention in our world, over and over again. The presence of God's cloudy-fiery pillar of guidance was their constant experience. Daily they gathered the manna that He miraculously provided. His anger had flashed out at them in their disobedience; His love had healed again and been their constant shield. *These men and women had a direct, personal, visible, and constant experience of God as no other generation has had!*

But now they were about to pass over the river Jordan and enter a land that God had promised their fathers. While God would still be with them, when this generation passed away and left their children in their place, there would be no similar experience of God for *them.* Instead, God has given His Word—the commandments and statutes and guidelines for life on which the society of Israel was to be built. In the future, God was to be known through His Word.

So it was vital that Moses show this people, poised on the edge of the promised land, *how* they could pass on the reality of relationship with God to their sons, and to their son's sons. And it is here that we find the Bible's central statement for believing parents—a statement that helps us understand how *we* can communicate the reality of a personal relationship with God to *our* children, through the Word that He has given us.

Obedience. It's clear that in this communication, obedience *is* important. Three times the passage says, "Do them," "Keep [them,]" "Be careful to do [them.]" But, strikingly, the urgent insistence on obedience to God's Word is not presented as an end in itself! "Do them . . . that your days may be prolonged." "Do [them] . . . that it may be well with you." *Obedience is urged because it is the pathway to blessing for the believer!*

This is an important thing for us to realize about God's Word. He speaks it to us because of *love*. God knows that you and I are unable to tell what is truly helpful in life or what will hurt us and others. We cannot tell, so God tells us. He gave us His Word: He says, "This is the way, walk in it" (Is 30:21). And the path His Word marks out is the way of safety and joy.

In this view of the "commandment," we see a Father's heart revealed. We see a Father who wants what is best for His children and who thus takes the toddler's hand to guide him over the rough places in the path toward home.

Sometimes we warp obedience out of this context. We fasten on *obey* as an end in itself. But when we see the rule or command apart from its purpose, we lose sight of love. Then God becomes Someone we cringe back from, who doesn't care about *us,* but just wants us to do what He says—or else! Such a distortion can slip into our own homes if we come to feel that our main task as parents is to "get" our children to obey. That obedience itself is the goal. Then we become people who insist that our children do what we say because we say it. We demand *purposeless* obedience. And when we demand purposeless obedience, we are not acting in love!

When we do this, we step out of the pattern provided for us by our heavenly Father, and become petty tyrants who try to *rule,* not guide.

Love. Love is first seen in Deuteronomy 6 as the motivation God has in speaking His commandments and His guiding word to us. But love plays an additional role here. Love, not obedience, is the real goal toward which God guides His children! "Obey," Moses told God's people, "that it may be well with you." But the culminating command and call? "Hear, O Israel . . . love the LORD your God."

God's goal for us is that we love Him. How fully the rest of Scripture echoes this thought. When asked the law's greatest commandment, Jesus responded, " 'Thou shalt love the

Lord thy God' . . . This is the first and great commandment.
And there is a second like it: 'Thou shalt love thy neighbor as
thyself.' The whole of the Law and the Prophets depends on
these two commandments" (Mt 22:6-40, Phillips). And so
Paul agrees with His Lord: "The end of the commandment is
[love] out of a pure heart" (1 Ti 1:5, KJV).

God's great goal is not that people should *obey* Him. We
might obey those we hate if we fear them enough! God's goal
is that we might *love* Him and then be moved by love to
obedient response. God's goal for us focuses on our heart;
our innermost motivations rather than our overt behavior.
And so must our concern as parents focus on the motives, the
attitudes, the values, the *character* of our children.

We can see why. Chuck was a model child, as long as his
dad was around. But when his father was away on one of his
frequent business trips, Chuck was uncontrollable. He refused
to listen to his mother, he teased his brothers and sister, he
shouted and disobeyed.

Kent was always quiet during his high school years. He
went to church. He dated infrequently, studied hard. He was
pleasant, softspoken, cooperative. And then Kent went away
to college.

Chuck and Kent are not unusual, are they? You know children and young people just like them. And you wonder why.
For Chuck, it was a stern father who kept tight rein on his
oldest child and always insisted on instant obedience. Chuck
obeyed—as long as Dad was there. *He conformed to the behavior his father demanded.* But those behaviors were not an
expression of his growing character! When Dad was gone
and the force Chuck respected was removed, his behavior
changed. All the hidden antagonisms and bitternesses spilled
over.

Kent had never been or even felt very rebellious. He had
simply fitted into his parents' way of life. He accepted it as

his own; he did not really know any other. But in college, he was suddenly submerged in a world of new experiences, different life-styles. And Kent, because his behavior too had been conformity rather than an expression of his own character and decision, changed.

Chuck and Kent illustrate why "obedience" is an incomplete and inadequate goal for parents to set. You and I will not always be with our children to see that they behave as they should. When we are not there, their behavior will spring from what is in their hearts, from their character. And so what a parent must care about is just what God cares about—character, the heart. What we must seek to nurture, just as God seeks to nurture it in us, is *love*.

A glimpse

Certainly the glimpse we've seen of God's goal for His children is incomplete. The New Testament adds much to our understanding of what it is that God wants to do in us, and in our children. But the glimpse we have here is enough to warn us away from several dangers.

First, obedience is a poor measure of parental success. In fact, some of the things that parents do to gain obedience actually block the development of love and Christian character!

Second, if I take my pattern for parenthood from God, I realize that I have to be very conscious of my own motives when guiding and setting rules for my child. My commandments, like God's, need to be purposive: first, for my child's good, and, ultimately, to teach him to love God.

Third, my task as a parent is to work with God in shaping the heart and awakening the love of my child for the Lord. Certainly this involves more than teaching right beliefs, more than insisting on right behavior. And because it does involve more, I desperately need to see how God uses me in my children's lives. I need to know from His example and from His

Word how to perform a task I am unequal to—yet called and privileged by God to undertake—to lead my children toward life's great goal.

You will gain most from this short book if you stop with me at the end of each chapter to react—and act.

REACT

1. Does seeing Bible commands as **purposive** make a difference in the attitude of a person to whom they are directed? If so, what?
2. The author says that the goal of **obedience** which many parents set in bringing up their children is inadequate and can actually be harmful if it is seen as a primary goal. What reasoning supports this statement? Do you agree with it or disagree? Why?
3. Study John 14:15-24.

ACT

1. On a piece of paper, write out the goals that you have for your children; that is, what do you want to help them become, and be?
2. Now on another paper, write the last five commands you can recall giving your children. Check each to see (a) what was my attitude when I gave it? (b) what purpose did this command have? (c) how did it most likely affect the attitude, the heart, of my child?
3. From the above: How was I like or unlike God in my role as a parent?

2
Your Heart

One phrase in Deuteronomy 6 stands out
boldly, and states the primary prerequisite for
parents who hope to shape the lives of their
children toward the Lord. It's simple! So
short that we might tend to overlook it. Yet it is
so basic that we **must** begin our ministry
as parents here and nowhere else. "These
words, which I am commanding you today,
shall be on your heart" (v.6).

The November trip to Michigan was long and cold, and both my 12-year-old and I were unusually quiet. We pulled into the driveway of the home I had known as a child, and when I saw my dad standing stooped by the old garage, tears filled my eyes.

In two short days I stood in the Milan funeral home and conducted my first funeral—my mother's. During those days my son Paul had been very quiet. He had come to the funeral home once, briefly, to sit motionless in a chair against the wall. Then, later, he had shaken his head when asked if he wanted to come down again. Now Paul sat beside his grandfather and his aunt in the front row, as a sea of faces stretched back and filled even the overflow room.

I remember the strain before the service began, then the peace during the service, and a true surge of joy as I looked toward the flower-burdened casket and realized fully that my mother was not there: she was with the Lord she loved, far more *alive* now than when I had last spoken to her and felt her touch.

That night as Paul and I settled down in the attic room that had been my room as a teen, his bed was shaken by the first sobs to break his quiet those three tense days. I sat beside him, put my arms around him, and told him that I had cried too— and I shared with him the joy I had known in the confident assurance that mother was not really *dead,* but that she lived, and that we would see her and be with her again.

Later I told Paul, who had been very close to his grandparents, that it was just so that he might cry, and be comforted, that I had brought him with me to Michigan. And I realized that it was only because God had made the great joy of eternal life so real to me at the funeral that I was able to communicate it to my son.

He had grasped, and felt himself, what was in my heart.

For good, or bad

It is a basic principle of human life that we communicate what is in our hearts to our children, for good or bad. "Children copy their fathers," the Bible begins, taking as a starting point for a crucial exhortation a fact commonly recognized in New Testament days as well as in our own (Eph 5:1, Phillips). Somehow, it is expected that a child should be like his parents and bear in his character as well as in his form, some family resemblance.

I know this. But it still irritates me to see my own bad traits so faithfully reproduced in my own brood. One trait especially I can trace back to my days in grade school. There we were ruled by a fearful principal, a stern five-foot-two, who was the terror of us all. One of his rules was, No hats on in school. You can imagine then the sudden fright that gripped me when I saw the principal bearing down on me one day as I stood in the hall with my cap on! Quickly, without even thinking, I snatched off my cap and marched up to him. "Mr. Drevhdal, can you tell me where to buy a Christmas tree?" He looked at me for a moment, then said, "Yes, Lawrence. Right down the block there at Squires, the corner you pass every morning on your way to school."

I said, "Thank you, sir," slipped out the school door, put on my cap, and was away.

I used to look back on this little escapade with some satisfaction, until I discovered that my children too are quick to seize on all sorts of creative ways to wriggle out of tight corners. They find it so very hard to admit any fault.

Somehow I succeeded in communicating what had been in my heart—even when I didn't want to.

Modeling

Sociologists today speak much of the processes by which what is in the heart—the core of the personality—is transmitted to others. The processes by which likeness is communicated are most often spoken of as "modeling" or "identification." These are far more than mere imitation. DeNike and Tiber suggest that:

> Identification is a process in which a person believes himself to be like another person in some respects, experiences the other's successes and defeats as his own, and consciously or unconsciously models his own behavior after him. . . . The fact that there is emotional involvement with the other person distinguishes identification from mere imitation.*

Wherever there is close emotional involvement, as in the parent-child relationship, there will be modeling and identification. And others have pointed out that where the child is loved by the adult with whom he is identifying, and his needs are being met by that person, there is strong reinforcement given for that process to take place.

Strikingly, identification is a process that focuses on what we *are,* not what we *say.* I may say to my son, "I value honesty, and want you to admit it when you've done something wrong." But if he sees me attempting to excuse my errors rather than honestly facing and admitting them, he will do what I *do*—not what I say.

This is why God has given us the great prerequisite, His great warning: "These words . . . shall be on your heart." Before we can lead our children to love and obey God, we ourselves must be loving and obeying Him. We cannot say to them "Do this!" if we are not doing it. In their love for us, and response to us, they will instinctively fasten on what we are, not what we say, and their character will become like ours.

This is another compelling reason we cannot expect the

*L. Douglas DeNike and Norman Tiber, "Neurotic Behavior," in *Foundations of Abnormal Behavior* (New York: Holt, Rinehart & Winston, 1968), p. 355.

church to bring up our children as Christians. We may take our boys and girls to Sunday school, and they may hear the words of truth there. But it is the word of truth that they see in our lives that will be communicated! They will become what we are.

Not perfect, but growing

It is something of a shock when this truth first comes home to us: our children are becoming what we are.

It is a shock, because none of us is perfect. "In many ways we all offend" (Ja 3:2). And as we look into our lives and our hearts, we realize there is a great gap between what we ourselves want to be, and what we are. Does this mean that we can *never* be effective parents—particularly since it is in our youth that we have our children, long, we often feel, before we have time to grow toward maturity in Christ?

It is good that God understands us. He knows full well that we are not perfect, that we have not "arrived." And so His task for us is not based on our being perfect. Instead, He wants us, as imperfect creatures, to share with our children the reality of living our life with Him: the reality of *growing* in Him. Perfection is not required for this. But there are other requirements.

Life. The Bible tells us clearly that all men, while they have physical life, are empty of a life they need to make them complete: eternal life. We were made in the image of God (Gen 1:26-27), and while that image was marred and distorted in the fall (Gen 3), we still bear it (Gen 9:6). You and I and other people are God's supreme creation, shaped to be like Him as living, loving, persons. But when sin entered the human race, and man died spiritually (Eph 2), the capacity to be truly like God was lost. And so was the possibility of living life to its fullness. So the Bible pictures us as "spiritually dead all the time that you drifted along on the stream of this world's ideas of living," following "the impulses and imaginations of our evil nature," and thus strangers to all we had been created for (Eph 2:1-3, Phillips).

No matter how intelligent, how moral, how effective in business or personal life an individual may be, as long as he possesses only created (or physical) life, he is a husk, an empty man—a man who is not fulfilled.

But breaking across the bleakness of this dark picture of man comes God's gospel—the good news that Jesus Christ brings us *life,* that real life which God intended for us. "I am come," Jesus said "that they might have life, and that they might have it more abundantly" (Jn 10:10, KJV). The Bible says that "even though we were dead in our sins God, who is rich in mercy, because of the great love he had for us, gave us life together with Christ" (Eph 2:4-5, Phillips).

With this new life from Christ, all that man is potentially again becomes possibility.

We are no longer bound by our inadequacies or our sins. We can reach out and touch God, and be touched by Him. And He can work His change in our personalities, teaching us to love Him, guiding us to obey Him, and in the process make us different persons—with different values and attitudes and feelings and ideas that are more like His own.

It is important to realize, as we face this task of being good parents that *we must have this new life from Christ first*—before anything.

We communicate what we are.

If we are dead in sin, what can we communicate? Death. And sin.

If we are drifting along on this world's ideas of living, what can we communicate? This world's ideas of living. A drifting goallessness.

If we are following the impulses and imaginations of our evil natures, what can we communicate? Only what we are.

What we can never communicate is the reality, the freshness, the abundance of a new and eternal life we do not possess.

So the first thing each of us has to do is ask Do I have eternal life? Do I have Jesus Christ, in whom and with whom the Bible says I can find life?

How good that the gospel is so simple and so available. God states it clearly. "Go so loved the world, that He gave His only begotten Son" (Jn 3:16). God loves us. He gave His Son. And as history testifies, that Son surrendered His life on an executioner's cross. Jesus died, and in death brought us life.

There is much more in the Bible—about *how* His death brings life; about why it had to be this way, and no other; about how death was unable to hold Jesus, and He broke its bondage in a glorious resurrection. But what we need to appropriate is God's love—His promise, His assurance that Jesus' death was enough. That now we can find eternal life in Him. And, fastening on the centrality of Jesus and the forgiveness He brings us, we need only to put our trust in Him. "God so loved the world, that . . . whosoever believes in Him [His Son] should . . . have everlasting life."

You can begin new life, everlasting life today—now—by simple trust in Jesus.

Then, having God's new life within, you do have something to share. Something besides death and frustration and failure to communicate to your children. You have life!

Growing life. When we accept and receive the life that God offers us in Jesus, the Bible says we are "born again" (Jn 3:3). What an appropriate picture. We have new life—a new birth from above—but it is a baby's life. Our personalities are encrusted with the old ideas and values and attitudes, the old feelings and ways of reacting to other people, that were built up during our years of living as the dead.

Now there is a new life within us, struggling to express itself. The rest of our lives, that life will grow in us, struggling to force out of our personalities all that is of the old, the sinful, the merely human. All our lives will be spent in discovering more and more of what God's life is like, as we see that life reflected in Jesus and recorded in the Scriptures and being experienced by us!

What this means is a simple thing. Being a Christian means to grow, and to change. It does not mean to be perfect.

This is an exciting thing to realize. I am never to communicate perfection to my child, or even attempt to! The Bible says that we all sin, and that failure to recognize and admit sins, and confess them to the Lord, breaks our fellowship with Him. The same passage suggests that we are to live with others just as we live with God—openly, honestly, confessing, relying on forgiveness and love to maintain relationship (Eph 4: 25-32). So we *can* be "good parents!" Christian parents, *if we are growing Christians,* and if we let our children see us, not as perfect, but as *seeking to grow.*

And so we return again to the words of our passage. "These words which I am commanding you this day shall be on your heart." As we open our hearts and lives up to the words of God, as we seek to grow in Christ and in conformity to His words, then we do have something to share with our sons and daughters.

We have life, and we can communicate it—for we communicate what we are.

We love God's Word, and we can communicate love for His words. We communicate what we are.

We are growing toward Him, toward a life patterned on His words. We can communicate this desire to grow, this desire to live Jesus' way.

We communicate what we are.

REACT

1. The author suggests we can be effective parents without being perfect, but letting

our children see us as imperfect people who are seeking to grow more and more like our Lord.

How does this concept make you feel? Why?

2. Often traits and attitudes that we develop in our childhood and youth are not the ones we want. We want to shake them off. God's gift of eternal life in Jesus is the basis for change, for freedom to become different.
What two conditions does this chapter suggest must be met if you are to be able to change? Have you met them?

ACT

1. Study Matthew 5:43-48, to see there two kinds of love—one patterned after this world's ideas of living, the other on God's ideas of what life is all about. Jot down ways each of these kinds of love might be expressed in relationships you have with specific individuals.

2. Analyze your relationships with the individuals you thought of in 1, above. Which kind of love does your life actually express? What, then, do you expect to be communicated to your children?
Can you see why it is so important that God's Word be upon **your** heart if you are to be an effective Christian parent?

3
Life-linked Words

We can explain the appearance of many traits that show up in our children in simple social-psychological terms. They "catch" their ways from us through natural processes which are recognized by all, if not fully understood. And there is nothing wrong with the believer admitting that God works through these natural processes to do His work in human life. It's simply that we need to remember, **there is more.**

In Deuteronomy 6, God directs our attention to the central role of love: love motivates His speaking to us; love for Him is the source from which our obedience springs. God invites us to know and love Him, and our primary task as parents is to lead our children into love for the Lord.

But before we can lead our children to love God, we must love Him. So first of all, His words must be in our hearts, settled down deep in us and forming the core of our own personalities. With God's love, God's Word, shaping and transforming us, we have something compelling and real to share with our boys and girls, our young teens and seniors.

With this said, God goes on in Deuteronomy 6 to explain more fully how we communicate what is in our heart—how we share with our family the reality that we have found. At this point, we turn to the words of God themselves, the content of His written revelation, to see how words are linked to life. And the pattern God presents? "These words which I am commanding you this day shall be on your heart; and you shall teach them diligently to your sons and shall talk of them when you sit in your house and when you walk by the way and when you lie down and when you rise up."

Living words

Too often we treat Scripture as though God gave us His Word simply to be heard and accepted as true. In the days of the prophet Ezekiel, there were many people who loved to listen to God's Word—and who were judged for it! God told Ezekiel,

> Your fellow citizens who talk about you by the walls and in the doorways of the houses, speak to one another, each to his brother, saying, "Come now, and hear what the message is which comes forth from the LORD." And they come to you as people come, and they sit before you as My people, but they do the lustful desires expressed by their mouth, and

their heart goes after their gain. And behold, you are to them like a sensual song by one who has a beautiful voice and plays well on an instrument; for they hear your words, but they do not practice them. So when it comes to pass—as surely it will—then they will know that a prophet has been in their midst. (Eze 33:30-33).

What a graphic description. They come. They sit before the prophet as God's people. They hear. They hear what is said. *But they will not do it.* And because they hear but *do not do,* the Word of God has no impact on their lives, other than to bring them to judgment.

This is the striking thing about Scripture. God has not given us His word only to hear—or even to "believe"—but primarily to *do!*

This theme is emphasized over and over throughout the Old and New Testaments. "Be ye doers of the word, and not hearers only, deceiving your own selves" (Ja 1:22, KJV). "If you abide in My word, then you are truly disciples of Mine," Jesus said (Jn 8:31). And the wise man, who hears Jesus' words and "puts them into practice" (Mt 7:24, Phillips), is the one who builds his life on the solid rock. But the man who builds on shifting sand "hears these words of mine and does not follow them" (Mt 7:26, Phillips). There is something about Scripture that calls, not for mere acceptance, but for action.

We gain insight into what this is when we look at the Hebrew and Greek words for truth, and realize that both testaments insist, "Thy word is truth" (Jn 17:17). The underlying idea here, the reason God's Word is dependable, is that it reveals *reality,* as opposed to mere appearance.

Suppose you were walking down a path and came to a narrow bridge spanning a gorge with a river far below. The bridge appears sturdy, but there is a sign there saying, "Danger. Rotted timber. Keep off." What will you do? If you

judge by appearances, you will probably ignore the sign. But
of you judge the sign trustworthy, you will read, *and do what
it says*. If the sign fits the reality, the only appropriate thing
to do is to heed it, and act accordingly.

This is just the case with the Bible. We live in a world of
swirling appearances; this appears desirable, that appears
good, this appears helpful, that appears uncomfortable. Yet
underneath all the appearances of this world there is a reality:
there is that which is truly desirable, truly good, truly helpful,
truly wrong. It is the ministry of the trustworthy Word of
God to serve as a sign, warning us away from the harmful,
pointing us to the good. We are not to be *entertained* by
Scripture; we are to heed it and, by our obedience to it, to
stake our very lives on God's trustworthiness.

God's words are to be lived.

Too often we treat the Bible as though God's words were
empty, rather than full of truth. How? By hearing—but not
doing. In Ezekiel's day, God's people loved to come and hear
the prophet speak, and with their lips they showed much love
(Eze 33:31). But their hearts were set on a different path.
While they heard, they would not do.

When we live like this, all we can share with our children
is the emptiness we ourselves know. We can transmit to them
the Bible's content, but we will fail to communicate God's
words as reality. They may well grow up to be orthodox, but
God cares first about the heart.

It is just this: this treating God's living words as dead
words, that the Deuteronomy passage guards against by out-
lining a *living* pattern for our teaching.

Lived words

In an anthropological study of education in Taleland, Mayers Fortes contrasts a way of learning which he calls "training" where ideas or skills or concepts are taught in a classroom
context, with a "real life" approach.

> The training situation demands atomic modes of response;
> the real situation requires organic modes of response. In
> constructing a training situation we envisage a skill or ob-
> servance as an end-product at the perfection of which we
> aim and therefore arrange it so as to evoke only motor or
> perceptual practices. Affective or motivational factors are
> eliminated or ignored. In the real situation behavior is com-
> pounded of affect, interest and motive, as well as perceptual
> and motor functions. Learning becomes purposive. Every
> advance in knowledge or skill is pragmatic, directed to
> achieve a result then and there, as well as adding to previous
> levels of adequacy.*

What he is saying is of greatest significance for us as we think
about communicating God's Word to our children. When we
learn something as an item of information, isolated from the
life, our inner feelings and motivations are not touched. When
we learn something in real life—when we learn in a situation
in which we see truth being *lived,* fleshed out with the feelings, motives, and behaviors that are appropriate to it—then
learning becomes purposive, and we touch the heart as well
as the head.

This is just what God's Word has told us for thousands of
years! "Teach my words diligently to your sons . . . talk of
them when you sit in your house and when you walk by the
way and when you lie down and when you rise up." The context in which God's Word is taught as living words is *real life
itself*—not a classroom where Bible ideas are heard, but their
meaning not demonstrated in experience.

When we grasp this great fact, so much of what the New
Testament says takes on fresh meaning. To Timothy, a young
man Paul trained in the ministry, the great apostle says
"You . . . have known intimately both what I have taught

*Mayers Fortes, "Education in Taleland," in *From Child to Adult,*
American Museum Sourcebooks in Anthropology, ed. John Middleton,
(Garden City, N.Y.: Natural History, 1970), p. 381.

and how I have lived. My purpose and my faith are no secrets
to you. You saw my endurance and love and patience as I
met all those persecutions and difficulties at Antioch, Iconium
and Lystra. And you know how the Lord brought me safely
through them all" (2 Ti 3:10-11, Phillips).

Timothy *knew* that the words of God were truth. He had
heard those words, and seen them proven true in the experiences he had shared with Paul. And so Paul says in another
place, to another people, "Be imitators of me, just as I also am
of Christ" (1 Co 11:1). No wonder in writing to Timothy
Paul said, "Pay close attention to your self and to your teaching" (1 Ti 4:16), and even so echoes the order of priority
seen in Moses: "[My] words . . . shall be on your heart; and
you shall teach them diligently" (Deu 6:6-7). First the heart,
then the words of teaching.

The fact that we are to communicate God's truth as *lived
words* gives us many insights into how we can best teach our
children. God is not demanding that we reproduce the classroom in our home. Far from it. The classroom too often iso-
lates words from their lived meaning. No, we are to use the
Word of God to explain our daily actions and to illuminate
our feelings: to "talk about them" during all the shared experiences of daily life.

Recently we hired a workman to do some work around our
new home, and agreed on a price. After taking several advances for the supposed purpose of getting supplies, it became
clear that he was in fact defrauding us. Suddenly all sorts of
trouble boiled up around him. His partner stole money and
broke the partnership; he was sued over a previous job; his
wife filed for divorce and locked him out of his home. Within a few days, he was literally and completely destitute.

We had talked of the situation at the dinner table, and how
we wanted to relate to him. We could hardly afford the loss
of several thousands of dollars, or trust him any further. Yet
we asked God to help us care about *him,* rather than the

money, and to use us to show this man Christ's love, especially when we learned of his troubles. And God answered our prayers. Of everyone he had known, all others turned against him. And as I rode one day with him in his pickup to get more supplies for the job, he told in tears how, until we agreed to work something out with him, he had felt that even God must reject him. Somehow our concern helped him to realize that God would not reject him, but cared.

Within a few days, at a local church to which he was invited by some Christian acquaintances, he went forward to receive Jesus Christ as personal Saviour.

We could, in a class, have discussed for hours the Scripture that says, "Love your enemies, bless them that curse you, do good to them that hate you, and pray for them which despitefully use you, and persecute you" (Mt 5:44, KJV). But that word of God became *real* for the family when, together, we lived it and linked our actions to this command of God which love had moved us to obey.

Life-linked

The thoughts we have just traced help us understand, then, just what the task of the parent is in Christian nurture, and why the Sunday school and other church agencies can never replace the home in God's plan.

Scripture is by nature *living* words. It is not enough to learn them, to accept them. We must live them.

Scripture portrays reality as we are to experience it. This is why the Word is to be lived rather than just understood. God's Word probes beneath mere appearances, and shows us how to live godly lives. How to rely fully on His trustworthiness and grace.

To communicate *this kind of word* adequately, we must first be living it ourselves, and then verbally interpret our attitudes and actions to our children, as we share daily life with them.

It helps us to realize this. It helps to realize that while we *can* learn Bible stories and biblical information as a classroom exercise, to be felt and to be accepted as reality, Bible truths are to be seen in and heard from one in whose person they are being incarnated. We can sum up the impact of this understanding in a simple way.

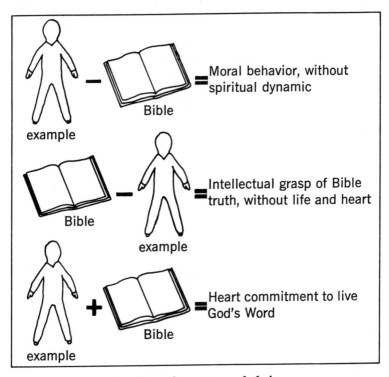

Patterns of nurture and their
product

If we provide a moral example for our children, without linking our actions and attitudes to God and His Word, as the wellspring of our behavior, we may well produce moral persons—but persons without spiritual dynamic, who neither know nor love the Lord.

If we teach the content of Scripture without its incarnation in our own lives, and without showing by our actions and attitudes our love for God and commitment to the reality He has revealed, we may well produce persons who are "orthodox"—but who will not *do* God's Word, and will have no vital relationship with Him.

But if we provide an example of commitment that flows from the fact that His Word is in our hearts, *and* if we relate our attitudes and actions in real life to His words, thus showing God to be the source of our personalities—then we will see develop persons whose hearts are open to God, and who will be ready to respond in obedience to Him.

This last statement may seem presumptuous. But it rests on God's promise. "Train up a child in the way he should go, even when he is old he will not depart from it" (Pr 22:6). For God has shown us how to bring up our children His way. He has shown us that we are to love God, to keep His words, and daily to show the relationship of what we are and do and feel to the words that guide us.

It is in this way that living words are shown to be truly infused with life, and it is in this way that hearts are opened to the God who speaks them.

Summary

In these first three chapters, then, we have looked at basic principles that help us grasp our role as Christian parents. These principles are not meant to be "practical," if by practical one means to spell out specific do's and don'ts. But the principles are the foundation of all our practices, and it is our practices as we minister life in our homes that we will look at in the next section of this book.

In brief review, these are the principles our practices and our understanding of the parent's task must rest on.

Our goal as parents is to lead our children to a love for

the Lord, a love that is expressed in obedience to Him (cf. Jn 14:15-24).

Before we can communicate this kind of faith to our children, His words must be in our own hearts. We must know Him, and be growing in our love for and obedience to Him.

With His words in our hearts, we are to share them with our children and teach them to our children as we live them. This means that we both *show* our children the reality of God's living words by doing them daily, and also that we point to the words of God as we respond to them, and so teach our children that they learn in "real life."

When we build our practices on these principles, when we take them seriously, we can see why only parents are able to share God's Word as a truly living Word with younger children, and why even teens need the living example and guidance of their parents far more than anything the church or peer group can provide.

"Teach them diligently to your children."

Thus God has said. Not, "See that someone teaches them." But you. *You* teach.

Teach a *living* word.

REACT

1. What makes the difference between treating Scripture as dead words and living words?

2. The chapter section, "Lived words," suggests that there is a critical difference between words which are taught in the classroom and that which is taught in real life. Can you write down, without looking back, what it is that makes the difference? Check your answer against the text.

3. How would you answer a person who objects to what is said in this chapter "be-

cause the Holy Spirit is the One who teaches and opens hearts"?

ACT

1. On page 32 the author gives an example of a situation in his home where the family sought to respond in God's way, and to verbally relate actions and attitudes to God's Word.

   Can you recall times in your recent experience where you linked your actions and attitudes to God's Word, and thus shared a living word with your children?

   Jot down brief descriptions, and share them in discussion with your husband or wife.

Part 2
PATTERNS FOR PRACTICE

*You have forgotten the exhortation which is addressed to
you as sons,*

> *"My son, do not regard lightly the discipline of the Lord,*
> *Nor faint when you are reproved by Him;*
> *For those whom the Lord loves He disciplines,*
> *And He scourges every son whom He receives."*

*It is for discipline that you endure; God deals with you as
with sons; for what son is there whom his father does not
discipline? But if you are without discipline, of which all
have become partakers, then you are illegitimate children and
not sons. Furthermore, we had earthly fathers to discipline
us, and we respected them; shall we not much rather be
subject to the Father of spirits, and live? For they disciplined
us for a short time as seemed best to them, but He disciplines
us for our good, that we may share His holiness.*

Hebrews 12:5-10

All of our life together is a discipline, a training and shaping of our personalities for our good, that we might share
God's holiness. "Discipline" is not "punishment." Discipline
is guiding, shaping, training, molding, sharing. Discipline is
being involved in one another's lives, and especially in our
children's lives, for their good.

4
Heart to Heart

It's too bad that **discipline** has such an overtone of harshness, of "punishment." While discipline in any home will at times involve use of external sanctions, the whole meaning of discipline is much closer to "guidance" than to "punishment."

Even when we look at passages of Scripture in which the element of chastisement is present, as in Hebrews 12, we have to remember that this teaching presupposes a context, a climate of relationships that is stressed throughout the New Testament. Any kind of discipline is effective only when the relationships within the home are marked by honest affection and love.

God describes the climate in which Christians are to live this way: "Let all bitterness and wrath and anger and clamor and slander be put away from you, along with malice. And be kind to one another, tender-hearted, forgiving each other, just as God in Christ also has forgiven you. Therefore be imitators of God, as beloved children; and walk in love, just as Christ also loved you and gave Himself up for us, an offering and a sacrifice to God as a fragrant aroma" (Eph 4:31-5:2).

The climate of the home is to be one of love, of tenderheartedness, of forgiveness.

There is a vital reason for this. We saw in the first part of this book that God wants to work through us to touch the *hearts* of our children. This is the first reason that His Word is to be in our hearts. Then we are to share His words with our families as we ourselves live them in real life. We are to communicate the reality of God, heart-to-heart.

We have all known since childhood that there are such things as conductive metals. Some metals, like copper, carry an electrical current from one place to another without themselves being seriously affected. Other materials, such as rubber, are insulators. These materials will not carry a current; they will block its passage.

If we carry over this notion of "conductor" and "non-conductor" into relationships, we discover that the Bible teaches us that *love* is *the conductor along which heart-to-heart communication can flow.* An atmosphere of love is essential for reaching the deepest personalities of other persons: without love, they are insulated from us and from whatever we might try to share.

So when we begin to think about the practical things that make it possible for the divine principles to work out and take flesh in our homes, we need to probe for the meaning of love, and how to build a climate of love in our relationships within the family.

Love is kind

This is a simple thought that reflects a verse most toddlers learn in Sunday school. "Be ye kind." It is so easy to grasp and to remember. Love is kind.

But it is not as simple or straightforward as it seems. For this idea is filled with troubling implications.

Interpersonal. Love is not something that can exist in isolation from people. Love exists in relationships between persons. Yesterday my wife and I were talking about a passage in 1 John, a passage that says "The one who does not love his brother whom he has seen, cannot love God whom he has not seen" (1 Jn 4:20). On the surface, it seems hard to accept this. We all know it is *much* easier to "love" someone far away—someone you don't have to live with and rub up against and find irritating or upsetting. It's so easy to "love" the poor object of missionary effort overseas—and to ignore the neighbor next door.

But this is just the point! A man can *say* "I love" without *loving.* He can talk, and think, and even believe that he feels love. But real love is not in words or feelings—real love is in action. And so the Bible says, "Love not with word . . . but in deed" (1 Jn 3:18). Love exists as reality only where there is a relationship in which it is being expressed.

Involvement. This too is implied. Love is concerned. Love reaches out to care for another, to become involved in his or her life.

We know from Jesus, who told us to love "just as I have loved you" (Jn 13:34, Amplified), that love is a reaching-out kind of thing. "We see real love, not in the fact that we loved God, but that he loved us and sent his Son to make personal atonement for our sins. If God loved us as much as that, surely we, in our turn, should love one another!" (1 Jn 4:10-11, Phillips). And so the Bible sets love in clear focus. Real love is not put off by the attitudes or even antagonisms of others,

any more than Jesus' love drew back from the cross because
we were sinners and would not first love Him. Love reaches
out to become involved in others' lives—and to care.

Consideration. Love is *kind.* Love looks to the needs of
others, and seeks to meet them. For kindness seeks to understand and consider the feelings and situation of other persons.
Kindness is an expression of love which can be *understood* as
love.

And this is a hard thing. So often love is misunderstood.
Often we do things out of love, but the things we do are un-
wise. For years I rose early to clean house for my wife, who
is allergic to house dust. I thought of it as an act of love. She
felt it as an implied criticism of her inability to be a "good
housekeeper." For years she looked for an expression of love
that would involve a deeper sharing of my feelings and
thoughts than I had been able to provide. Did I have love,
and express it? Yes. But it was not a *kind* love. It was dumb
love, love that did not understand or consider the feelings
and attitudes and needs of the other. It was a love that was
not considerate.

"Love is kind" looks so simple on the surface. But as we
live in families, as we see our children appear and grow, we
learn that building a climate of love—real love—is not an
easy or an automatic thing.

We have to grow together in our ability to express the reality of our love in our interpersonal relationships, establishing
and maintaining real involvement in each other's lives, and
expressing our love in truly kind, truly understanding ways.

Mom and dad

Building and maintaining a climate of love in the home
begins with the relationship between you, the parents. While
it is so easy for our relationships to break down, so easy for
little strains and misunderstandings to interrupt heart-to-heart
communication, the Bible does show us specific practices that

will help us live together in considerate (rather than "dumb") love.

Open hearts. Communication of love, as of faith, is a heart-to-heart thing. So it is essential that the communication lines be kept open, that neither partner is closed off from the inner-most personality of the other. Sociologists tell us that children need to be exposed to what they call the "inner states" of adults. This simply mirrors a biblical insight: "Who . . . knows the thoughts of a man except the spirit of the man, which is in him?" (1 Co 2:11).

We object to this. "Can't she *see* I love her? Doesn't she know I don't mean it *that* way?" The answer is no. She doesn't know. She cannot really "see" that you love her by your actions alone. Only when you express your thoughts and emotions and your motives will she know your heart. *Then* your actions will take on meaning. Then they will be seen as acts of love.

This is what God, the Father to whom we look for example, has done with us. He has gone beyond His mighty acts in his-tory—gone beyond what He has done—to *explain in words* what was in His heart when He created, when He disciplined, when He gave His Son to die. We see the love revealed in Christ's cross. We understand it as love because God has opened His heart to us, and shared Himself with us in words.

Sometimes we have a hard time grasping this. We think our partner ought to know what's going on inside us, intuitively. And so we don't say anything—we do not explain—we do not reveal—and then we are hurt when we are misunderstood. *But no one can really understand anyone simply by seeing what they do.* We need to share what is inside us, that com-plex of feelings and attitudes and understandings from which actions flow. We need to learn to live with our families with open hearts.

This is how Paul lived with those in the Christian commu-nity. This is an essential ingredient in building a climate of love. "Oh, our dear friends in Corinth," Paul cried, "we are hiding nothing from you and our hearts are absolutely open to you. Any stiffness between us must be on your side, for we assure you there is none on ours. Do reward me (I talk as though you were my own children) with the same complete candor!" (2 Co 6:11-13, Phillips).

Do you want to have a climate of love in your home? Begin by opening your hearts.

Seek reconciliation. Christians are human. Sometimes we forget this, or pretend to. We try to live with each other as though we were perfect, and at least should pretend to be. When strains come—when we hurt each other, or strike out at another, or close ourselves off because of a sin or weakness that hurts too much to reveal—we find a sense of alienation easily slips in.

God's Word speaks directly to such situations. "If your brother sins, go and reprove him in private" (Mt 18:15). Usually we try to ignore a hurt or wrong. We bury it inside us and pretend we aren't wounded. But it *is not* all right. That hidden hurt is a barrier between us; a block to openness. Such things can lie deep within us, and begin to fester until they breed the bitterness and resentment that can spoil a marriage (cf. Col 3:19, Phillips).

If you feel wronged, the Bible says, go to your partner and seek reconciliation.

But this is not all. What if you are the one who caused the hurt? What if the anger, the striking out, the wounding, was by you? If so, Jesus says to you, "If therefore you are presenting your offering at the altar, and there remember that your brother has something against you, leave your offering there before the altar, and go your way, first be reconciled to your brother, and then come and present your offering" (Mt 5:23-24). How urgent is reconciliation? Jesus puts it first, so vital one should even interrupt worship!

So both the one who feels wronged, and one who wrongs, have the same duty: seek reconciliation. Go to the other person. Settle it now in order that with the blockage in your relationship removed you might continue to live together with open hearts.

Forgive. When a person goes to another to "reprove him," he is to go with a particular attitude. The reason for going and bringing the painful issue into the open is not to convict the other, or hurt him in return. The reason for going is to let forgiveness wash out the pain and restore harmony.

The Bible says, "Why, then, criticize your brother's actions, why try to make him look small? We shall all be judged one day, not by one another's standards or even our own, but by the judgment of God" (Ro 14:10-11, Phillips). We do not bring things out in the open to judge or to condemn or to criticize.

We bring things out in order to be reconciled.

This goal gives us real insight into how we are to approach someone who has wronged us, or whom we have wronged. We are not to focus on what they did but on how we felt!

To say, "Bob, that was a mean thing to say. You were trying to hurt me!" involves both judging Bob's motives, and attempting to make him admit guilt. It's an attempt to *force* him to apologize.

How different it is to say, "Bob, when you said such-and-so, it really bothered me. It made me feel so small and worthless." This approach does not attack, it reveals. It is an opening of the heart, an evidence of trust, and a demonstration of confidence that the other person will respond, in love.

It is that pattern of trust and forgiveness, quickly given and received, that Scripture says we are to develop. It is tenderheartedness: "forgiving each other, as God in Christ also has forgiven you." If we fail to forgive and accept forgiveness, we must resort to closing our hearts and to manipulating one another. It is with open hearts that we can give and receive love.

Care. Caring really sums it all up: the motives in which we reach out to each other, the ways in which we express love. "Walk in love," the Bible says, "just as Christ also loved you, and gave Himself up for us, an offering and a sacrifice to God" (Eph 5:2). We are to give "much love and sympathy" (Col 3:19, Phillips) to *really care* how another person feels and how we can help.

When openness, desire for reconciliation, a free giving and receiving of forgiveness, mark our lives together, then in our homes we will have that atmosphere of love which is the ideal conductor of God's Word.

The little ways

A climate of love in the home is a big thing but expressed in little ways. Love is really listening to another person, to discover what he thinks and feels. Love is putting the other person first, trying to see things from his point of view. Love is slowness to lose patience, looking for a constructive way to build up rather than to tear down. Love doesn't try to impress, or hold inflated ideas of one's own importance. Love is even seen in good manners, in courtesy. It isn't touchy; it doesn't look for slights or insults in what others say or do. Love trusts and keeps on trusting.

So let us live with each other, loving in these little ways, seeking God's help to experience in our relationship the openness and care His Word encourages. When we do, our home will become a place in which the reality of God and His words will be communicated to our children—heart-to-heart.

To some concepts, reaction and action are appropriate. For others we need to go beyond, to take definite steps of evaluation and implementation. The concepts dealt with in this chapter involve that kind of need—and the activities suggested here are designed to help you meet it.

PROJECT

For husband and wife

Do each of the following individually, then sit down and compare your responses. Remember, as you compare, the importance of openness and of trying to see from the other person's point of view. Remember too the importance of concern.

Doing this project together should help you evaluate the present climate of your home, and should also help you enrich and deepen your relationship.

1. Jot down the things you do in order to show or express love for your spouse.

2. Make a list of the things he or she does that you see and experience as expressions of love.

3. Jot down any things that you believe your spouse may not understand about you and your feelings. Also record what makes you feel he or she does not understand.

4. Often misunderstanding and hurts or resentments spring up secretly in marital relationships.

    (a) List anything that you feel is a barrier, or cause of alienation, that affects your present relationship with your spouse.

    (b) Look back to page 47, and **write out** how you would tell your spouse about these barriers **without attacking** him or her. That is, write out how you would open your heart without judging or condemning.

    (c) Can you think of anything that you might have done that has hurt or injured your partner? How are these to be handled (see p. 46)?

5. On a continuum chart such as the one below, put a check where you believe your home is now.

OPENNESS

We live   We are open
hidden lives.   and free with
                                                    each other.

UNDERSTANDING

We misunder-   We know
stand each other.   each other
                                                    fully and well.

CLIMATE

We are cold,   We experience
unloving.   the biblical
                                                    ideal.

(At least one day after doing 1-5, begin this section.) The last page of the chapter lists a number of "little ways" in which love is expressed. List these, and together check through 1 Corinthians 13 and Philippians 2:1-5. Compare several New Testament paraphrases.

Then take each trait and discuss how fully you are experiencing it together. Don't hesitate to share when you feel there is a lack, and be specific in pointing out what it is that makes you feel the lack. But at the same time, don't hesitate to share the positive, and express your appreciation and thanks for each "gift of love" your husband or wife does extend.

If you want to go on, you can explore the area of personal relationship by reading together and discussing an appropriate book or books, such as the Moody Press books **How Do I Fit In?** by Larry Richards, and **You and Yours,** by Ellen McKay Trimmer.

5
Family Unity

When children come, the climate established
by husband and wife envelop them. They
breathe the atmosphere created by their
parents—of love, or of tension.

It's often difficult for parents to help their
growing children into the kind of relationship
that they have with each other as adults.
During the terrible twos, when "no!" seems
to mark off the toddler, the ideal of treating
the child as a person may dissolve under the
realization that a two-year-old does not act as a
person should. So life with a 2-year-old often
becomes a contest of wills.

But through all the growing years, through
all the changing times, parents need to
work for the kind of harmony and unity that
mark the home where Christ's love is lived,
and real.

Each year in my Christian home course at Wheaton College
I asked my students to isolate what they remember about their
homes as "good." What, to them, speaks most clearly of unity
and stability, of a healthy climate in which they could develop as persons. The answers have remained the same year
after year.

Here is what college students recall as most important.

"My parents loved me." "I always knew they cared for
me, even when I did something wrong."

What so many speak of in these ways is *unconditional love.*
Unconditional love contrasts totally with the kind of love
other guys and girls reported: "I felt my parents would love
me as long as I did what they expected. But if my grades fell
or I did something wrong—" This "if" kind of love is *condi-
tional love.* It's based on performance. It is "I will love you
if you earn my love, but if you do not earn it, I will reject
you."

No one is perfect: every child falls short of his parents
(and his own) desires in so many ways. How important to a
growing person's sense of worth to realize that, even when he
has fallen short, he is valued and important and loved.

Christ shows us the pattern of unconditional love in the
story of the prodigal son. How striking that this is far more
the story of the constant father, the father who continues to
love his child even when the boy has strayed far from him
and his precepts.

Unconditional love is God's kind of love. It does not excuse sin, but it never rejects the one who falls short.

"My parents always showed respect for my opinion." "From
the time I was young, I was given responsibilities and helped
to meet them."

This is another factor that is always mentioned. College
students who looked back on childhood and adolescence at
home agreed that a mark of the good home, the Christian

home, is that parents show *respect* for the feelings and ideas and capabilities of their sons and daughters.

Respect can be shown in a number of ways. Some parents give their children an allowance when they are very young, teach them how to spend it wisely, as they grow, increase the allowance to include clothing and other personal items. Some parents develop a family council, where the ideas of each family member are considered in planning for the group. Still others give their children responsibilities, increasing them as they grow older—responsibilities that are not just "jobs" but meaningful contributions to the family's life together, the kind of thing that a young person has satisfaction in successfully accomplishing.

Actually, the ways respect is shown vary tremendously. What counts is that some young people are aware that their parents seem to trust them, and want to help them make more and more of their own decisions. What counts is that they *feel* their parents respect for them as persons in their own right.

"My parents and I always talked a lot." "I felt that if I had a problem or a good time, I could always share it with Mom (or Dad)."

This doesn't mean that the young people did talk everything over with their parents. But they always felt free to.

A sense of openness in *communication* is a tremendously critical thing, a thing on which many of the other factors hinge. We have already spoken of communication in the last chapter. It takes place heart-to-heart: it is marked by the open heart, the eagerness for reconciliation and harmony, the free flow of forgiveness. This is involved in the feeling of freedom some children have to share with their parents. When Mom and Dad are open and honest with them, when Mom and Dad set the pattern by sharing their feelings and listening with concern and interest when their children share, the sense of freedom grows.

There can be no unity without communication: there will
be no communication without the awareness that each cares
for the other and shares his real self with them.

Sometimes parents feel that they should relate to their
children as an authority figure (something we will look at in
a later chapter). In any parent-child relationship, an adult
must still be an adult. But each (adult and child) must be
persons to the other. A cold, distant insistence on one's *right*
as a parent to demand that your child always do or feel as
you say he must will lead to communication breakdown. Such
a parent may bring his child to compliance, but such a parent
will not touch his heart and nurture commitment.

So it is important—to us, and to our children—to listen,
and to share. It is important to take time to talk.

"My parents had clear standards for themselves and for
me." "I saw in their life the commitment to what they said
was important."

Young people resent it when parents expect behavior and
attitudes from their children that they don't expect of themselves. Many collegians report that they do not know what
their parents' values really are, that they cannot tell because
they did not speak of values, and their lives show no commitment to something that makes life meaningful for them.

Really, unity is built around a *core of common commitment*. Jesus said that we would find our oneness in Him and
in His Father (Jn 17:21-23). This is true for the family as
it is for the church. When we have a commitment to Jesus and
His words, and when we live that commitment, our children
can build their lives, with us, around a common core. Without
a common core there can be no unity.

Fragmentation

It may seem strange to write about the "good Christian
home" in which family unity is developed as parents express
unconditional love and respect for their children, and in which

there is not only a consistent parental example but also a free flow of communication. It seems strange, perhaps, because today sociologists are talking about the breakdown of the American family and its fragmentation.

Many families are separated by work, as Dad works long hours, or Dad and Mom work different shifts. Many historic functions of the family in past years have been shifted from the home. Recreation is now something that school programs take care of, or that neighborhood clubs provide. Religious training is something that happens in church, where parents and children are shunted off into carefully graded programs and isolated activities. Education is taken care of by the public school system, and with the new math, we poor parents can't even help our second graders any more! Some suggest that the family is so divided, so seldom together, that its members simply cannot understand each other's problems and interests! More than one person has pointed out that when the family *is* together, it is usually before the TV screen, with talk limited to superficial remarks passed during the commercials.

Is it possible in a world like ours to even think of developing family unity?

Nothing new. In looking at this problem, we need to begin by realizing that while the specific things that compete for family time and attention may be different today than in the past, competition is nothing new.

An evening school student of mine, an adult in his late forties, wrote about his childhood—long before TV and other modern pressures.

> When I was a child we didn't do much together, that is, with our parents. There were three of us in the family, and we were left up to our own activities. I remember once that we went to the zoo together. It was fun at the time, but we only did it once. It would have been nice to have gone to a

ball game or two, or to have gone on a picnic or two, or
have gone on a hike or fishing. These are outdoor games,
but I would have liked to have seen us do some things at
home together, such as checkers, etc. But none of us were
home long enough to enjoy things together, so I can't say
too much more.

It is not technology that cuts into our family life. It is the
priorities that each of us sets.

Take Jack, who owns a gas station, and works six days a
week from 7 A.M. to 6 P.M., and often stays on to work ex-
tra hours. Jack and his wife also have church commitments,
that take one or the other of them away from the home three
or four nights a week, and as Eileen says, they find it tempt-
ing to treat family time like ironing—something that can always be pushed into the closet for next week.

Still, they spend Sunday afternoons together, staying home,
or going for a ride, or going swimming in the summertime.
Other times, they putter around the garden, which has proved
to be a real source of family togetherness. Jeryl, the four-year-
old, helped plant the seeds while Daddy opened the furrows
and Mother covered them. Then, during the week, when Daddy gets off work, they all go out of the house "like old farm-
ers" to look things over or pick something for supper. In the
evenings, they roughhouse on the floor. The two little ones
(they also have a 14-month-old boy) enjoy "pounding" Daddy. And sometimes they go shopping together, getting something to eat out afterward.

Life isn't ideal for busy Jack and Eileen and their family.
And it will be harder as time goes on, and they discover that
older children require even more time.

But family life need not settle down into a whirl of evenings away from the home—by Dad, and Mom, and later by
the kids. Family life need not settle down into evenings sitting
in front of the television, with time only for the empty

shadows on the screen while the flesh-and-blood persons beside us grow away from us.

Priorities. The fragmentation of our time and our families is something that imperceptibly seems to erode the quality of our family life, until we awaken with a jolt and discover that we have become families of strangers.

This need not happen to us. *But it will happen if we fail to take conscious action.* To prevent this we must set priorities now, and make choices on the basis of values we have chosen.

Some years ago, University of Chicago professor Richard J. Havighurst suggested that either parents simply do not care about the persons their children will become, or they simply will not tolerate the frustration of their own selfish interests that is involved in guiding a child to become a self-respecting individual. His comment is still appropriate today. Too many of us do not care, or are unwilling to make the effort involved in building a Christian home and family life.

But we can, if we will.

Years of change

As a child grows, his needs and interests and capacities change. And the ways that we communicate the things we have been talking about—extending of unconditional love, showing respect, setting standards, keeping open communication lines—these change too.

This is why no one can say, "This is what to do to have family unity." Our practices and emphases shift with the growth and change of our children.

Babies. To babies, love is communicated in many ways, but primarily by touch and tone of voice. Babies under six months require no discipline, no training. But they do require love: handling, cuddling, talking to, laughing with. It's easy to give time to a baby: they're lovable. And it is vitally important that from a child's first days he senses the warmth and the intensity of our love, shown in every possible way.

Toddlers. Toddlers are sometimes hard to love! Over, under, around, and into everything—exploring, often testing and retesting the limits we set for them. Toddlers too need love and attention, cuddling, sitting with and looking at pictures while "reading" a book, going on special walks to explore the wonders of God's world around you.

Toddlers also need limits. One way we show respect and love for children of this age is to set important limits for them, but to also realize and respect their need to explore. Too often a pattern of relationship is set during these hectic days—a pattern marked by Mom or Dad constantly saying no to everything a child does—trying to change a child into a "little adult" long before he is capable of behaving as anything but a child. Such overcorrections result in children coming to feel that they can safely ignore parental instructions. It is such a burden to attempt to enforce the unenforceable that parents who do overcorrect only punish at times, when they blow up after a string of little irritations.

Showing respect for your child at this age means recognizing his characteristics, and realizing that—irritating as he may sometimes be to you—he *needs* to crawl and explore and to pry. Treating him with respect means setting some limits. "Don't touch Mommy's dishes in that cabinet. They'll break." But also let him do what will not harm himself or others. Treating a toddler with respect also means that, while you firmly restrain him when he moves to break the limits, you explain (over and over again) why the limits are set. "Don't touch. The pretty things will break." Your toddler probably will not understand the words you use, but he will understand that you have reasons for your limits, and that you respect him enough to explain.

Your children. To the patterns of life you have established when your child was a preschooler—patterns of expressed love, of purposeful limits and explanation for enforced limits and rules—you now have much to add. You have listening when he comes home from school, looking at his papers and projects, displaying them on a family bulletin board. You have special things he can do—cleaning his room, putting his clothes in his own laundry hamper and bringing them regularly to the washroom, setting the table. You have story-books you can read together—books from school, and Bible story and other Christian books for his age. You can plan family outings, and he can take part in planning as well as in going. You can find so many, many ways to show him that you care about what happens to him, and what he is interested in.

Adolescence. With the teen years come fresh opportunities. You can find new ways to increase his freedom of choice, things he will be able to handle because you worked toward this time by giving him an opportunity for decision making when he was younger. You can do more things together: you can communicate on a deeper level, for his capacity to understand and consider things in an adult way is growing. And you can step up into wider adventures in living: wilderness pack trips, shared sports and hobbies. When the pattern of communication in the home is kept open, building on what has been done in the early years, there need be no "generation gap" in your home. You will listen to and respect him, and he will listen to and respect you, and he will respond to your authority when you point out that in some areas you have to decide as one responsible to God.

Throughout the growing years, each dynamic factor in family life can be expressed, in different and appropriate ways, and the personality of your child can be built toward the time he will leave you to launch out on his own life with the Lord. In the home where unconditional love, mutual respect, open sharing, and a common commitment to biblical values mark the relationships of family members, there need be no fear for the present or the future. "Train up a child in the way

he should go, even when he is old he will not depart from it"
(Pr 22:6).

Being together

There are many other things that contribute to family unity.
There are ways of living together that help establish a sense
of security and safety. Central to them all is the idea of *being*
and *doing* together. We may work together. Some of the
closest times I have had with my teen have been in work
projects we have shared. We may play together—a trip, a
fishing expedition, an afternoon in a canoe, or simply a walk
through stores to look at and talk about the things that interest
us. We may sit around the table together, to play a game like
Pit. We may develop our own family traditions: like our tradition of a midnight, Easter family communion. And our Christmas tradition, when for ten days before the date remembering
the Lord's birth we light one more candle each night, and
read from Scripture the words of light and life His incarnation
brings us.

Surely, it is easier to do it ourselves. We adults can get jobs
done so much faster. We can shop more quickly. We can
plan more effectively. But it is important for unity that we be
together, do together, talk together, share together.

And unity is important.

It is vitally important that we sense our oneness, our love,
and our respect for each other, and that we open up our lives
and share.

REACT

1. The author suggests that many modern
   pressures tend to keep families from being
   and doing together. List some things that
   make it hard for your family to be together.
2. There are four keys to relationships in the
   home that are critical for unity. List these

from memory. Then check back over the first section of this chapter to see how well you did.

3. Divide a sheet of paper into two columns. On the left, list actions that communicate or express these four qualities (see 2 above) positively. On the right list actions that seem to violate each.

ACT

1. Go back over the list of pressures you made for 1, above. Which of these is more important to you than your family? Which can be handled by setting a priority that limits your involvement?

2. Visit a Christian bookstore and pick up one of Marion Jacobson's books on family fun and recreation. Make up a list of things to do from it, and talk over with your children which ones seem to them most fun. Make plans to do some.

3. If your children are adolescents, ask them to read this chapter and talk with you about the atmosphere in your home. How do they see the state of each of the four critical areas? How could you—and they—help your home atmosphere to grow and improve?

6
Good "Discipline"

So far in this section we have been thinking about the context of relationships in which a child can best grow toward maturity. Now it is time to focus on specific methods for dealing with discipline: the practices a parent can use in guiding his children toward the righteousness which is God's goal in disciplining us (Heb 12:10).

There are no simple rules we can follow in every situation. But there are guidelines.

Earlier, I suggested that we need, in general, to think of
discipline as teaching, guiding, explaining, supervising, and
directing a child's choices. I also suggested that we need to
keep our goals in discipline clearly in view: we want to in-
ternalize values so that a person's character is shaped rather
than his behavior merely controlled. Thus, many writers stress
the need for remembering that discipline is "not just obedience." It is the inculcation of a desire to do right when parents are not there. It is, ultimately, the development of a self-
disciplined personality.

As we move now to focus on specific discipline practices for
the Christian home, let's try to answer questions that commonly arise.

Why discipline?

Some years ago, many children were raised by a "permissive" approach. The notion was that good is rooted deep in a
child's personality, and that by removing external pressures
and restraints, the flower of his individuality will open un-
bruised and unblemished. The result? Unrooted persons, without self-discipline, constantly hurting themselves and others.

Today both secular and sacred writers approach the question of discipline more realistically. Neither take a permissive
approach, or believe that simply reasoning with a child, simply
helping him to "understand," provides sufficient guidance.
The secular writers explain the need for external and internal
controls in psychological terms. Unsocialized human nature
includes a mass of asocial impulses. If people are to live together, if life is to have direction, if a person is to feel right
about himself and to achieve in society, control over these
asocial impulses must be developed and maintained. And so
discipline is needed, first as external control, then as a growing capacity for self-control.

In theological terms, this "mass of asocial impulses" is
termed *sin*. The Bible gives no glowing picture of what we men

are in ourselves. While made in the image of God, and still of infinite worth and value, the entrance of sin has twisted the nature of man so that selfishness both rules and is expressed in man's impulses. Apart from discipline, we will always follow our impulses, and will harm both ourselves and others. Thus we need to provide external control over the selfish expression of human needs and impulses until inner controls can be developed. Certainly the Bible agrees that such control is necessary for human society to function, and necessary if a person is to reach his potential as a human being.

But the Bible goes far beyond the suggestion that the home and society help a growing child control his asocial impulses. God wants to *transform* our personalities from within: to renew our minds and rekindle our love and redirect our wills through conversion and growing obedience to Christ. But even the new person that we become "in Christ" needs to grow, needs discipline and training.

So, whether our children have accepted Christ or not, they continue to need our guidance and our direction, and our help in learning to control the sin which struggles to express itself in their lives and distort them.

What is bad discipline?

Sometimes in attempting to guide and control, parents do a poor job. They discipline badly.

Basically, anything is bad discipline which does not help us achieve discipline's goal—when it does not in fact provide for the child needed control, and when it does not facilitate internalization of values.

Let's consider three critical factors that most often seem to characterize bad discipline.

Too harsh. Punishments are out of line with the nature of the "crime." It is unfair, for example, to restrict a child from playing with his friends for a week because he forgot to take out the garbage or make his bed. This kind of harsh discipline breeds resentment, not a desire to do right.

Too negative. If we understand discipline as guidance, we can see why we need to emphasize positive alternatives to undesirable behaviors. You have a child who keeps on knocking over his milk glass. Too negative discipline might involve continual warnings: "Don't knock over your milk." "Be careful!" "Watch out!" In this setting, the best discipline might simply be, "Carla, if you set your milk glass down behind your plate, instead of by the edge of the table, you probably won't knock it over again."

Too personal. Bad discipline tends to focus on the person, not the problem. "You bad girl, you knocked over the milk again! Why aren't you more careful? Oh, you just *won't* listen to me will you, you bad girl!"

Ordinarily with children, we want to skip over the error or wrong behavior, or touch on it lightly, and then go on to emphasize the positive alternatives. We want our children to discover the pleasure of growing able to avoid mistakes and errors, and to realize that they do feel good about themselves as they do what is right.

If we fall into the trap of disciplining in ways that are too harsh, too negative, and too personal, we will defeat ourselves. We will not help our children grow in their desire to do right. This kind of discipline flows from the selfishness and vindictiveness of the parent's sin nature: it is not an expression of God's love or of His ways of dealing with His children.

What is good discipline?

As we have been suggesting, good discipline presupposes, first of all, a relational climate like that discussed in chapters 4 and 5. Good discipline has its source in a good relationship, a relationship of honest love and expressed concern.

Within this relationship, nearly any discipline practice—from vigorous spanking through that look of dismayed disappointment—may effectively guide and control. It is true that research has shown a general correlation between the kind of relationship and the discipline practices parents tend to develop. The closer the relationship, the more love is shown, the less reliance there seems to be on whippings and spankings and threats. The less love is sensed and expressed, the greater the parents' use of power-oriented techniques—spankings and threats to force compliance.

There are times in any home where physical restraint and punishments, as well as other kinds of guidance, will be appropriate and best. Yet the practices that are most closely associated with discipline seem to be those that are naturally present in a love relationship. They are the kind of things that can be adapted naturally by loving parents. Let's look at six ideas specifically.

Show, don't tell. "Clean your room!" is something a child can quickly be trained to do as Mother shows him *how* to dust, to mop or sweep, to pick up and put away. There is a big difference in showing rather than simply telling.

Limit commands. As with the toddler, so with all children, rules and commands should be limited in number. Make rules about the things that are really important for you and your child. And see that the rules are carried out. But don't make rules about *everything.*

Also, when you want him to do a certain task (like washing dishes), don't make a habit of calling, "Charles, do the dishes!" You show respect for your child as a person by using a statement or request form of speech, rather than the imperative. "Charles, it's time to do the dishes." Or, "Charles, would you please come help me with the dishes now."

Explain; tell why. Another part of showing respect for a person's individuality is to explain the reasons for things they are asked or expected to do. This need not be an invitation to argument, and it will not be if you begin the practice early.

Explanation is an indication to your children that your love, like God's, is exhibited in purposive guidance and command.

Don't boss, work with. This is another important thing if you are to help your children integrate traits into their character. It is easy to be cast into the role of a boss. "Do this room now, and when I get home, I'll inspect your work!" Inspection can be a good thing, if its goal is to praise. God encourages us to respond in obedience to Him by reminding us that in the day of judgment our work will be examined. "And then each man's praise will come to him from God" (1 Co 4:5). But when we take the role of "boss," and the tone is one of criticism—"I'll inspect, to see what you did wrong!"—it is an entirely different thing. So we want to take time to work with our children, to show them how to do things well, and then to praise them for their accomplishments. It is important, that is, if we really want them to grow to be disciplined persons who will respond enthusiastically to God.

Relate punishment to the offense. Too often, punishment is related to our emotional reactions to their behavior, not to the nature of the offense. We will see later that punishment is a part of discipline, and has its own guidelines for effective practice. For now it is enough to note that when we punish, we should do it to the degree demanded by the offense, not according to the intensity of our feelings. This isn't easy. We need God's strength and wisdom to respond in His way. But He can give these, and will when we ask.

Be patient and consistent. Again, this is a challenging thing. For we are not God: our discipline is so often based on our reactions and feelings in specific situations. And we often make mistakes.

But our mistakes are not so deadly that they are likely to hurt the character of our children. Again, it is the atmosphere—the normal climate of the home—that is critical. When we really love, really listen, really share, then our lives will be marked by patience and consistence. It is this, the living out of the fruit of the Spirit with our families, that is the key to good discipline.

Is punishment good?

Punishment is, and should be, a part of discipline—but only a part. When punishment is needed, as part of a pattern of external control to teach helpful behaviors and attitudes while cutting off the unhealthy and wrong, we particularly need God's wisdom to punish well. For Scripture warns, "Don't overcorrect your children or make it difficult for them to obey the commandment," and again, "Don't overcorrect your children, or they will grow up feeling inferior and frustrated" (Eph 6:3, Col 3:21, Phillips). It is often in this area of punishment that we fall into the trap of overcorrecting, and make it difficult for our children to obey. So let us look at some of the factors that make punishment a good and healthy element in our whole pattern of discipline.

Stress natural consequences. Punishment should not be used as a club, to provide control through fear. The best kinds of punishment flow as natural consequences of children's actions.

"Jim, it's half an hour until bedtime, and you have to get in thirty minutes of practice on your trombone!"

"But Mom! My favorite TV show is coming on!"

"I'm sorry, Jim. But you've had all afternoon to practice And you knew you had to get in thirty minutes today. I'm afraid you'll just have to miss your show this time. Maybe you can plan your time better next week."

Does Jim experience his practicing as punishment? Surely! But it is just one of many unpleasant things that can happen when we put off, or fail to do, something we know we have to. How much better for Mom to be firm and insist Jim follow through on his responsibilities than for her to become upset and shout angrily at him about his failure to practice earlier.

Natural-consequence punishment is goal oriented, and a vital part of discipline.

Consistency. Many studies suggest that consistent and lenient discipline is far more effective than consistent harsh or inconsistent harsh discipline in controlling behavior. We should set as few rules as possible, striving to let children's ways of living be shaped by our example and our teaching rather than by rules. But when rules are stated or understood, they should be consistently enforced.

"Don't touch the glasses," when disobeyed, can be met with the physical removal of the toddler and a gentle, firm spank. But when the next time the child touches the forbidden glasses his behavior is simply ignored, a very poor pattern is being established. If there is something a child should not do at a particular age, then he should not do it, and we need to be consistent in correcting and punishing violation of the standard or rule.

Clear explanation. Involved in the above is the assumption that a child's misbehavior is related to something that is actually wrong, something for which there is a reason. Along with consistent discipline should come explanation of why punishment is given, and why the rule has been made.

Consider motives. It is important that when we punish we consider motive for a bad behavior as well as the behavior itself. Three-year-old Carol drops a cup in the sink, where Mommy is washing dishes, and it breaks. Should she be punished for breaking the cup? Not if she has not been taught not to touch them, and was merely trying to help Mommy with the dishes!

Fit the individual. Children differ, not only by the characteristics of their particular age, but also as individuals.

One child may respond to your tone of voice, another may need physical restraint. One may be punished effectively through spanking (we found a Ping-Pong paddle made an effective tool) with lots of noise and little lasting pain, but another may be better punished by banishment to his room. Sensitivity to each child, recognizing each as an individual and seeking to understand and train each in the best way for him, is an important part of all training.

Consider love-oriented techniques. I mentioned that we have used a Ping-Pong paddle in our home for spanking. I ought also to mention this is used infrequently—and now that our youngest is 10 years old, it has not been needed at all for several years.

Actually, reliance on power, on physical punishment, or on yelling or threats or personal attacks like "You really are no good at all, are you!" are ultimately ineffective and self-defeating. At best they produce compliance, and often lead to open rebellion. Love-oriented techniques may involve physical punishment at times, but they also will involve revelation of your own disappointment and, if you are hurt by a particular lapse, expression of your feelings of pain. And love may be expressed in each of the ways we have looked at in this chapter.

When the way we live with, guide, and even punish our children helps to maintain awareness that we love and respect them as individuals, our punishment and our overall training will move toward the big goal that we have for their lives.

Summary

Good "discipline," then, is really a function of a good parent-child relationship. When you, the parent, guide and direct and help your child make good choices, when you support him through example and praise and love-oriented punishment, you will be helping him discover the reality that underlies the words and ways of our God.

REACT

1. Review the discussion of this chapter and write your own paragraphs on factors the author did not develop, but which are important for good discipline.

   What is the role of praise in discipline? What impact does a parent's attitude have on how correction and punishment are received by a child?

   How important is understanding a child's motives for behavior?

   What will happen to the child if parents fail to discipline?

2. List all the factors discussed in this chapter. Give, from your own experience as a child, as many positive and negative examples of each as you can think of.

   Now, from your experience as a parent, give additional examples.

ACT

1. With your husband or wife, think through the occurences of the past seven days and list **everything** that might be viewed as "discipline" in its broadest sense (see beginning of this chapter).

2. Now transfer from the above list to a chart like that below, every incident that involved correction or some kind of punishment. Record under each column heading information on how you felt and acted. When the chart is complete, use it to analyze your own discipline practices, and to see if there are areas when you need to make changes.

The discipline situation	My child's behavior, and motives behind it	My response, what I did	Characteristics I exhibited of good or bad discipline

3. Do together a study of Hebrews 12:5-13. If you were to model your disciplining on God's example as a Father, how might you improve your present practices? Which of your present practices seem most like His methods?

7
My Authority

"My biggest failing in our home is my lack
of firm leadership and decisiveness, so this
is what I made an effort to improve on
this week, and though it still wasn't what it
should have been, it did make a remarkable
change in our home. This week I have
made decisions and stuck by them."

This father is beginning to discover that
his authority as a husband and a parent is
rooted in his own behavior and character—
not in his right to demand obedience. It
is an important discovery for all of us to make.

The whole concept of authority is under attack in our culture. In it all, the nature of authority is too often left undefined. Underneath the clamor, though, it becomes more and more clear that what most think of when they hear the word *authority* is "the right to require obedience."

This actually is a valid secular definition of authority. In the secular world, what Romans calls the "power of the sword" is given to governmental authority that social order might be maintained, with evil punished and thus restrained (Ro 13:1-5). Secular authority and the ability to punish on which it ultimately rests, are necessary in society because men are sinners: left without external restraints, enough people would follow their selfish instincts to cause the society to break down. And it is power, the power to punish and to reward, that is the means by which this kind of authority is exercised.

No wonder so many of us think of authority as "the right to require obedience," and become concerned when government seems less and less willing to maintain high standards of right and wrong, and less willing to enforce the standards that have been set.

But it is important, when we begin to think of spiritual authority, to realize that we are *not* dealing with "the right to require obedience."

Obedience

In the first place, obedience is an inadequate goal for the Christian to set. Both spiritual leaders in the church and Christian parents in the home must set as their goal a growing love for Christ that will issue in an individual's free choice to obey Him. As parents, we must ultimately be concerned with commitment, not merely with compliance.

Require

The concept of requiring response, so essential in the whole notion of secular authority, also must be questioned. One can "require" obedience. But no one can "require" an inner change.

It is true that as parents we can enforce certain behavior. During childhood, this is an important part of guiding the growth of our children's personalities. But no one can force or coerce another to act *willingly*. In fact, the whole idea of coercion to require a particular action implies that the person being required is *un*willing! If he chose to act willingly, there would be no need to "require!"

So somehow the Christian's use of authority is intrinsically different from that of the secular authority. Spiritual authority seeks to *encourage a willing response*—not to require a prescribed behavior.

Rights

A third point of contrast is focused in the idea of one's *right* to require obedience. It is appropriate for the secular authority to insist on the right to require. This right might be defended, if society is to remain viable.

But in the spiritual realm, while the right to lead is involved and does depend on God's appointment of an individual to leadership, the emphasis is on *responsibility* rather than on *rights*. The spiritual leader is responsible to lead. He does not "demand his rights," and become upset if someone doesn't obey. Rather, he recognizes his responsibility and seeks to lead in God's way so as to elicit willing obedience from those under his charge.

All of these contrasts are expressed in the Bible's teaching about spiritual leadership, teaching which we have recorded in the words of our Lord and His apostles. Once Jesus called His disciples to Him, and He said:

> "You know that the rulers of the Gentiles lord it over them, and their great men exercise authority over them. It is not so among you; but whosoever wishes to become great among you shall be your servant, and whoever wishes to be

first among you shall be your slave; just as the Son of Man did not come to be served, but to serve, and to give His life a ransom for many" (Mt 20:25-28).

And we hear this theme repeated by Peter:

I exhort the elders among you, as your fellow-elder . . . shepherd the flock of God among you, not under compulsion, but voluntarily . . . not for sordid gain, but with eagerness; nor yet as lording it over those allotted to your charge, but proving to be examples to the flock (1 Pe 5:1-3).

Whatever, then, the Christian's parental "authority" may be, it is an authority we must seek to understand and exercise as spiritual, not secular, leadership. Our authority does not focus on obtaining obedience. Our authority does not rely on coercion. Our authority is not so much a right to demand as a responsibility to exercise.

The servant who leads

The most striking picture of spiritual leadership in the New Testament is given by Christ: the Leader is a servant; the great One is a slave.

No picture could contrast more starkly with the secular notion of authority. Who is a leader? Who is a person with authority? Why, one who tells people what to do. One who insists that others obey him. One who insists that others respect his position and power. One who may be quick to punish and repay slights and insults, for he insists on his rights.

But a servant? Why, he does not command others—he takes orders. He does not tell others what to do—he does. He does not insist that others put him on a pedestal and look up to him; he moves *among* people rather than *over* them. He does not make people do things for him, he does things for them. He may suffer, but he does not repay.

Yes, the servant makes a peculiar leader—until we remem-

ber that the *goal* God has for spiritual leaders is to touch the
hearts of others, and bring them to a willing response to Him.
For this purpose, other methods than those designed to coerce
obedience must be used!

From Scripture, we can understand those other methods
and their dynamic, and we can see why as parents we must
adopt the role of the "servant-leader" if we are to exercise our
authority God's way.

The nature of the servant. Rather than being the source of
authority, a servant is one under authority. He is charged
with responding to his master.

It is important to note here that the servant is not necessarily under the authority of the ones he serves. The Bible
says that angels are ministering spirits, who serve us as the
heirs of God's salvation (Heb 1:14). But by no stretch of the
imagination are the angels under our authority. We do not
give them orders. They obey God.

So too a modern employee of a hotel may serve the guest
of the hotel, but remain under the authority of his employer.
The guest does not command the employee who serves him.

So the idea that as parents you and I serve our families
does not imply they rule us. Or that we ought to do whatever
they want. Our Master is Christ: our calling as servants is to
obey God and in obeying Him, minister to our loved ones.

Utterly central, then, to being a leader in the home is our
personal commitment to Jesus Christ, and our recognition of
Him as Lord as well as Saviour. My first duty as a parent is
to check out my own relationship with God. Scripture exhorts,
"With eyes wide open to the mercies of God, I beg you, my
brothers, as an act of intelligent worship, to give him your
bodies, as a living sacrifice, consecrated to him and acceptable
by him. Don't let the world around you squeeze you into its
own mold, but let God remold your minds from within, so
that you may prove in practice that the plan of God for you
is good, meets all his demands, and moves toward the goal of

true maturity" (Ro 12:1-3, Phillips). Only as I am consecrated to Him, being remolded by His Spirit from within, and
proving in practice that God's plan for me is good, can I hope
to *lead* my children.

In this we move back to God's command to parents long
ago. "These words which I am commanding you today, shall
be in your heart" (Deu 6:6). Our own self-chosen subjection
to God's will, and our own heart-motivated response to Him,
is the basis of our authority in the home.

We have no "right" to expect obedience from our children
when we ourselves are not obeying God. While we may require such obedience, our children's response will be at best
an external thing. Children copy their fathers. They will become what we are. Thus it is the servant's first task to obey.

The method of the servant. In saying that the leader is to
be a servant, Christ in no way suggests that he is not to lead.
The servant picture is a portrait of a *leader,* of one who has
and who exercises spiritual authority. The picture of the servant-leader is designed to make clear both the position of the
leader (as one who is himself under God's authority) and to
make clear the way in which he leads so as to gain followers.

The critical point here is that a servant does not lead by
telling others what to do; *a servant takes the lead in doing.*

At this juncture, we meet a host of New Testament teachings that support this point. Peter has written to leaders saying, "Shepherd the flock of God among you . . . [not] as lording it over those allotted to your charge, but . . . being examples" (1 Pe 5:2-3). The leader leads by doing and providing the example.

"As children copy their fathers you, as God's children, are
to copy him," Paul says to the Ephesians (5:1, Phillips). "Be
imitators of me," he says in another place, "just as I also am
of Christ" (1 Co 11:1). And to young Timothy, Paul writes,

> You, Timothy, have known intimately both what I have
> taught and how I have lived. My purpose and my faith are

no secrets to you. You saw my endurance and love and patience, as I met all those persecutions and difficulties at Antioch, at Iconium, and Lystra. And you know how the Lord brought me through them all (2 Ti 3:10-11, Phillips).

Paul, wholly committed to Christ, could say to his young disciple and to the churches, "Let me be your example." For Paul *was* an example—not a perfect man, but growing. Not sinless, but relying on God's grace, and constantly experiencing the work of God in his own life.

This is the central process by which we touch the lives of our children and exercise our spiritual authority. By providing an example, by matching the words of God and our own lives, so that our children might "know intimately both what we teach, and how we live."

This is the secret of spiritual authority.

The dynamic of spiritual leadership. Secular authority, as we have seen, rests for its effectiveness on power to coerce obedience, to enforce.

But no one can "enforce" a change of heart. No coercion can create a willing response. As I noted before, the whole idea of coercion implies that the one we have to coerce is unwilling!

So the dynamic of spiritual leadership and authority cannot rest in ability to coerce or power to demand obedience. This is why, when we think of discipline, that "punishment" really plays a small part. Punishment, and the power to punish, must be used wisely and in a limited way, or it is likely to produce rebellion.

No, the dynamic of spiritual leadership rests on processes that God has built into the nature of man, and on the working of His Holy Spirit in our hearts.

The processes God has built into human nature are noted in chapter 2 of this book. These processes are called by social psychologists by names like modeling, identification, and internalization. They do operate in each of us, and by them we all tend to accept and integrate into our own personalities the values and standards and behaviors of those we love and are closest to. God, Who made man, uses these natural processes which He built into human nature. As we live God's way with our children, He communicates His ways to them as a dynamic reality.

Yet identifying the natural processes does not give us even a partially adequate explanation of what causes a child or adult to respond to one with spiritual authority. For that explanation, we must rest totally on the sovereign and gracious work of God's Spirit in human hearts.

In Ephesians 5:21—6:9, Paul traces patterns that exist in the husband-wife, parent-child, and master-servant relationships. Summarizing then, he says, "Finally, be strong in the Lord, and in the strength of His might," for, he goes on, "our struggle is [spiritual] . . . against the world forces of this darkness" (6:10-12), whom, the Bible says, "is now working in the sons of disobedience" (2:2). Response to spiritual authority is a spiritual and not a natural thing: it is something only God can work, for only He can work to change a person's heart.

And so Christ encourages us. "My sheep hear my voice . . . and they follow me" (Jn 10:27). When we speak in His voice we *will* be heard by His children. And, again, "With gentleness correcting those who are in opposition; if perhaps God may grant them repentence . . . and they may . . . escape from the snare of the devil" (2 Ti 2:25-26). Jesus' people follow because they hear His voice. Those who oppose and resist will change, when God acts to free them from Satan's hold.

While recognizing the natural processes involved, the servant-leader lives out His commitment to God to demonstrate the reality of God's Word enfleshed, relying totally on God's working within the heart of the one he is responsible to lead.

Authority, then, in the spiritual realm is a very different thing from authority in the secular realm. The Christian parent, in seeking to exercise authority, turns away from the attitudes and methods and goals of the secular ruler, and seeks instead the life pattern of the servant. As a servant to his children, the Christian parent first of all commits himself to do God's will, and to be a living example of the reality of God. He does not "demand" obedience as an end in itself— nor does he use punishment to force a child to keep standards which he himself does not maintain! Only the man who lives freely under God's discipline can, in fact, bear the stamp of spiritual authority, and by his own example lead His children to choose God's will and God's ways.

Should Christian parents set standards?

It may sound as though one who exercises spiritual authority has no business insisting on right behavior from his children or others. But no such notion is implied. The Bible says that a child's responsibility is to obey his parents, even as adult believers are to respect and submit to those whom God has placed as leaders over them.

In Galatians, Paul uses an illustration that sheds much light. He speaks here of law, that expression of God's will as rules to be obeyed, and points out that law was necessary as long as men were "children." As children they needed law to act as a pedagogue, to enforce the will of the head of the family on those underage and thus not responsible. But, Paul goes on, when Jesus came and men were led from this childhood stage to become, by adoption, "true sons of God [adult, responsible members of the family]," then *inner* controls replaced *outer* controls (cf. Gal 3:23—4:7). As long as one is a child, and not responsible for his own behavior, he needs outer controls, and to be under another's direction and guidance.

So for parents, exercising spiritual authority involves di-

84   *You, the Parent*

recting one's children to choose and to do that which he himself does obedience to God.

In Thessalonians, Paul likens his own ministry to that church to the ministry of a father, and shows us more on how a parent guides his children.

You are witnesses, as is God himself, that our life among you believers was honest, straightforward, and above criticism.	*The example set*
You will remember how we dealt with each one of you personally, like a father with his own children, stimulating your faith and courage and giving you instruction.	*Personal involvement and direction given*
Our only object was to help you to live lives worthy of the God who called you to share the splendor of his own kingdom (1 Th 2:10-12, Phillips).	*The goal kept in mind*

When children and young people rebel, it is seldom because we have set standards or limits for them. Instead, it is usually because of the *way* we guide them—the way we act out the role of the secular leader who demands that others do things *his* way. No, we are to be spiritual leaders, who provide the example of commitment, and give personal instruction and guidance in living by God's will.

Is authority important in our homes?

Yes. Spiritual authority is important.

But this kind of authority does not exist as our "right to require obedience." It exists as our responsibility to lead our children by example as we instruct them in the ways of our God.

REACT

1. Compare the way these two parents are giving directions to their 9-year-old daughters.
   (a) "Clean up your room, Carol. And do a good job, not a sloppy one!"
   (b) "Ellen, it's time to clean up your room. Here's a list of the things you'll need to really do a good job."

   Which of these do you feel is acting in greatest harmony with the "servant-leader" role of authority? Why?
2. Reread chapter 6, and evaluate each suggestion concerning discipline in view of the nature of our spiritual authority.

ACT

Discuss with your husband or wife how each of you come across as spiritual leaders in the home.

1. Write down your own strengths and weaknesses.
2. Write down the strengths and weaknesses of your spouse.
3. Compare the two lists with your partner's.
4. Talk together about ways you can help each other strengthen your ministry as leaders.

8
Family Worship

"The way we think family devotions are to be done," says ten-year-old Beverly, "are like this. First we gather all six of us, and Father reads to us from the Bible. Sometimes he finds a book that he thinks is good for devotions. I like to listen to the stories. Next our father asks us questions on the story. After the questions, we pray. We all pray each time. Before we pray, we each tell our father what we want to pray about. Some of us pray for missionaries and some for people, that they will come to know the Lord. After we all pray, we talk some things over about the Lord, some things that we should remember and pray about next time we have devotions. I like devotions a lot. And it sure does tell you something."

Not every family finds time for family worship. Many who have tried have felt overwhelmed by problems, and every effort shortly seems to stop. Talks with dozens of parents about their problems show that these seven hindrances are most commonly mentioned.

Hindrances to family worship

Time. "The amount of time we have together as a family is very limited." "We begin, every so often, to try to set a special time for this in our home. My husband and I have felt that right after supper is the best time. We succeed to have devotions for a couple of times and then Billy has to hurry to eat as soon as Dad gets home, or even before Dad gets home, and then leave for Little League or Boys Brigade at church. The next night it might be me leaving for evening school, or Sheryl for Pioneer Girls or junior high church activities."

For busy families, "We'd like to, but we can't find time" is a common complaint.

Self-discipline. Closely related is the admission by many that they lack self-discipline. "We haven't succeeded in being consistent. Sometimes days and even weeks go by when we have forgotten all about family devotions."

Atmosphere. Others report that the greatest hindrance to devotions in their home is an unfavorable home climate. "When we argue with each other so much, how can we sit down and pray together?"

There is no doubt that lack of forgiveness, lack of concern, and a home empty of love will make it impossible to meet together in worship or sharing, except as an empty, legalistic ritual.

Inexperience. Many parents have never experienced meaningful times together in their own childhood homes. Oscar Feucht, the Lutheran family educator, comments, "Christian leaders are mistaken when they think their people have the 'know-how' of family worship. Actually, many adults do not know the simplest rules for reading the Bible meaningfully or composing their own prayers."*

Lack of participation. Beverly liked family devotional times. She liked listening to the stories, answering Father's questions, praying, and talking with the others about "things we should remember." Beverly sees herself as a participant.

Too often worship times are not something all family members can enter together. When members of the family are not involved, they soon lose interest, and devotional times drag to a halt.

Age differences. This is a serious problem which arises when children in the family range widely in age. Beverly's mother writes, "At our home we have four children, ages ten, nine, seven, and five. We're enjoying family devotions much more now than when our children were ages five, four, two, and zero, I can tell you that! Perhaps we weren't as well established in our Christian life then, or perhaps we tried to set a pattern that wasn't suited for such small children. I'm not sure. All I know is that it's not nearly as frustrating as it was then."

Trying to get the whole family to be together when some are young and others old, or all are very young, *is* frustrating!

Lack of meaning. Often this complaint is heard. "We just stopped. I don't know why, but we weren't getting anything out of our family devotions."

Are such times important?

In view of all the difficulties that parents face, we really ought to ask if family worship times are really important. Are they worth the effort they seem to take?

The answer, for many families, may well be no!

But before we give up the whole idea of family devotional

*"Christians in Families" in *Christians Worship,* ed. Oscar Feucht (Concordia, 1971) p. 103.

times, we ought to specify just when such times are not important or helpful.

Family devotional times are not important when the climate of the home is not one of love and of commitment to God's ways. We have heard it often in this book: faith is communicated life-to-life. When the relationships in the home are not Christian, when an atmosphere of love in which God's truth can be communicated heart-to-heart is absent, regular worship times will be empty and formal. These times may pass on Bible information to the child, but that will not be enough. If he does not see the reality of the words he hears in the lives of Mom and Dad, he may well reject what he hears as unreal.

Family devotional times are not important when they are formal times of communicating only information. It is vital that we know God's Word. But we need to know the Word in His way—as intimately linked to life, and thus vital and real. Reading a devotional from some book, offering up a prayer, without providing opportunity for family members to express their own thoughts and needs, soon robs worship time of meaningfulness.

Family devotional times are not important when they are forced into a rigid pattern of religious duty. God invites us to gather around Him, and to express our commitment to Him together. The heart of family worship is awareness of God's presence, and a desire to help one another respond to Him. Flexibility, variety, freedom to explore and respond to God in new ways, all these are marks of vitality in worship. When family devotions deteriorate into mere habit, devotional times are not important.

But, having noted the condition under which family devotional times are *not* important, let us go on to say that in the healthy Christian home, times for worship together *are* important—very!

In the Christian home, families are to live together in a climate of love. Parents are to be exercising spiritual authority by living Christ's life before their children, and by giving their boys and girls His kind of discipline and guidance. When we live together in these ways, we need time when we talk about our faith and its content—times when we make verbal and explicit our commitment to God, which alone explains the way we live with one another. Living God's life with our children is one part of communicating faith. Verbalizing the truths and values on which our lives are based is a necessary corollary.

The Scripture says we are to "talk about" God's words in our life together—as we walk, and sit, and go about the business of daily life. Much of our teaching should be done in just this way, informally. But we also need to sit down together, to share what is going on in our lives, and to link our lives at every truth with the Lord. If we fail to set aside times for this kind of sharing, we will find that we quickly fall into careless habits, and that the business of daily life crowds out thoughts and talk of the Lord.

It all starts with Mom and Dad

"Together times," for talking of the Lord and seeking His guidance for life, have to begin in the patterns of life set by Mom and Dad. As soon as a new Christian home is established, it is important for the young couple to set aside time to talk, to pray, and to grow together. Thoughts can be focused through a devotional book, or by reading the Bible together. One young couple describes their "nuggets of thought" method this way: "We chose the book of Hebrews, and beginning with the first chapter, read a short section of verses. Then we went back and took turns expressing what we thought each verse meant, taking time to meditate on the devotional meaning of the passage. When we didn't understand, we looked at different translations. In closing, we each prayed. We both have enjoyed this method."

Here both husband and wife are participants; both share.

Hopefully, each seeks also to share his inner world of feelings as well as his thoughts as God's Word probes and reveals. When there is openness between the partners, this simple method provides a framework in which meaningful interaction and learning can take place, and in which the Spirit of God can work through His Word in each life.

Even after children come, it is important for husband and wife to have "together times" of their own, times when they can talk, share, and explore God's Word for guidance. The climate of the home is set by the parents. Their closeness to the Lord and to each other is the critical factor in the nurture of their children. The family devotional times, aimed necessarily to the younger children, will not meet the special need that adults have for sharing together.

Family together times

When the family comes together for a devotional time, many of the principles discussed above apply. Particularly important is the realization that this is a time for sharing, for talking to and about each other, as well as about the Lord. It is a time when all we are and do is related and linked to the Lord and His teachings. Family "together time" is for sharing, for listening, for caring, for praising, for learning, for encouraging and helping one another love the Lord better.

Are there guidelines to enrichment of family "together time"? Here are a few.

Involve family members. One well-known Christian leader who is often away from home on trips leaves tape-recorded devotions behind. His family plays the tape at breakfast, listens to Dad's comments on a Bible passage, bows while they hear his voice praying, and then go off to school! The intention here may be commendable, but the method leaves much to be desired!

Family "together times" are times when the family is to share, and in sharing, link their lives to the Lord. Parents who want to involve family members can plan ways to encourage each to talk and share. When we feel we are participating, not being "preached at," we will develop the kind of feeling about devotions that Beverly expresses when she writes, "I like devotions a lot."

How can we involve family members? By encouraging them to talk about their day. By asking them to express their ideas and feelings about a verse or Bible story. By giving members responsibilities—make up a family prayer calendar and be the prayer chairman one week. In our home during the summers we have found that our youngest, now ten years old, enjoys special times alone with Mom and Dad. We plan simple times together using a notebook and a "study guide" that includes two questions on a selected Bible portion. The first question involves understanding what the passage says. This is written at the top of a page. The second question encourages thinking about its meaning, and opens out into all sorts of personal sharing. This is written halfway down the page. Timothy reads the passage aloud to us, then gets the first chance to answer the questions, and we all join in in discussion. Finally Tim records the answers he decides on in the notebook, and we pray together. Tim enjoys these times. We listen to him, praise his good ideas, and share our own thoughts.

For our teenager, regular family times come about 10 o'clock at night (we find the news too dismal to watch anyway), and usually these times involve each of us reading individually a scripture passage, then talking about it together. Sometimes we just talk—and consider these times of sharing and prayer as meaningful as our usual studies.

Fit interests and needs. Children at different ages have different needs and interests. So "together times" shift and change character as the children grow.

With preschoolers it is time for Bible storybooks with pretty pictures; time for talking about their Sunday school lesson and looking at take home pictures at bedtime. Little books like Mary LeBar's books for preschoolers soon become familiar favorites. Just being with a child at bedtime, talking quietly with him, praying with him as he goes to sleep, is important at this age.

As the children grow and go to school, their abilities and skills grow. Bedtime is still often the best time, unless the children are overtired. The quietness of sitting and sharing together makes a happy prelude to rest—far better than some exciting TV show to fill their nighttime thoughts and dreams!

Here, too, variety and flexibility are important. We have found that our children love the Jungle Doctor missionary books. Books by Ken Taylor (Children's Hour books, Moody Press) have also played an important role. Sometimes we have moved into creative projects. When Paul was in third grade, he was greatly interested in a story book about Robert Moffat, the Scottish missionary to Africa. So we made a "movie" of his life.

First, Paul talked about the scenes he would like to portray, and I jotted them down. After talking about the pictures that would best carry his idea, I bought a roll of paper about eighteen inches wide. Paul marked off forty squares, and began to draw in his scenes with crayon. We cut a hole in a cardboard box to make the screen, and then used two long cardboard rollers attached to each end of the paper strip to rotate and move the pictures across the opening. Finally, Paul marched up and down in front of my typewriter and dictated the dialogue explaining the pictures. I typed up a script using only his words, and then Paul read them onto a tape recorder, separating each scene with a bell as in a filmstrip. The finished project was an audio-visual report of the life and ministry of Moffat, which Paul later showed to his class at school, as well as to relatives at Christmastime.

Family devotionals, or together times, then, are not really

rigid rituals of reading and prayer. There is room for freedom and flexibility and for every-member participation.

Relevance. We have stressed this much. Together times are times to think and talk together about our lives and our Lord, times when we link our experiences to Him, and see how His words speak to us. Certainly, these are times when we grow in our knowledge of the Bible. But these are not primarily times for teaching: they are times for sharing, as relevant and as meaningful as life itself.

Bible times. There are a variety of ways the Bible can be explored during together times. Sometimes memorizing verses together can be fun. Looking up words in a concordance is enjoyed by third graders, who are developing language skills. Acting out Bible stories together, doing pictures of your favorite part of a story and explaining why, all these add fun and interest—and meaning—to Bible study.

Variety. Variety, keeping things flexible and different in some of the ways suggested above, helps to make family devotional times alive and meaningful to all. Planning ahead, changing approaches frequently, adding music and singing all help. But underlying the impact of family worship is the warmth, the closeness, and depth of the relationships that exist in the home. When that climate of love exists and is growing, when we are really interested in sharing the thoughts and feelings and ideas of each other, and when we honestly want to link our lives closely to the Lord—the family worship is an important part of life, and an exciting part for all.

PROJECT EVALUATE

For husband and wife (and older children, optional)

Do each of the following individually in preparation, then sit down and compare your responses. Remember the importance of openness and trying to see the other person's point of view.

1. Look over the section "Hindrances to family worship." Which are (or have been) the greatest problems for your family?
2. Jot down possible solutions to the problems. For instance, time. Is three times a week more realistic for you than every day? When is best? Morning? Bedtime? What would you need to do to set aside one of these times?
3. Recalling your past experiences in family devotions, jot down all the **positive** and **helpful** times you can remember. Then analyze. Is there anything that seems common to them? What has made family devotions most meaningful?
4. Think of each of your children individually and complete the following chart, sketching it out on your own sheet of paper.

Name, age	What does he/she like to do?	What skills is he/she learning in school?	What needs does he/she seem to have now?

5. Look over your chart again, and see if the information gives you any clues to answers to the following questions.

   When we have family devotional together times:

   —what interests of my child can I involve?
   —what abilities does my child have to participate? What are some of the things I could have him/her do to feel and be involved?
   —what Bible stories or concepts would be most relevant to my children just now?
   —how can I translate these ideas into specific plans to enrich my family's devotional experiences?

When these questions have been answered by each person, sit down together and talk over your answers. Be particularly concerned with trying to come up with positive suggestions in two areas: (1) what can we do to help each other grow as a couple? and (2) what can we do for family together times?

Next, visit a Christian bookstore. Ask about books and materials for children the ages of your own. Look too for materials that might help you as an adult.

Then, three weeks later, work through the project evaluation guide again. Have your devotional times changed? How? Talk each through again together as a couple, or if you wish, involve the whole family in thinking about the five question areas.

Part 3
THE DESIRED PRODUCT

For the time already past is sufficient for you to have carried out the desire of the Gentiles, having pursued a course of sensuality, lusts, drunkenness, carousals, drinking parties and abominable idolatries. . . . Above all, keep fervent in your love for one another, because love covers a multitude of sins. Be hospitable to one another without complaint. As each one has received a special gift, employ it in serving one another, as good stewards of the manifold grace of God. Whoever speaks, let him speak, as it were, the utterances of God; whoever serves, let him do so as by the strength which God supplies; so that in all things God may be glorified through Jesus Christ, to whom belongs the glory and dominion forever and ever. Amen.

1 Peter 4:3, 8-11

9
Commitment

The Bible sets the highest goal for us and
for our children. We are not to conform to
external standards: we are to be transformed,
that our love for God and others might flow
unfailingly and ungrudgingly. All that we
are is to be freely offered to one another for
Jesus' sake. And in everything, drawing
strength from the grace that our loving God
supplies, we have the privilege of glorifying
Him. For to Him belongs glory and dominion
forever.

We have said it often. The goal toward which parents must work is not conformity, but commitment. You and I are concerned with our children's character, not merely with their fitting into the mores of church or society. So we need to live with our children in ways that encourage them to choose God's values for themselves. We need to help them become persons who will joyfully apply biblical principles in everyday life. For this, our way of teaching and guidance in the home must touch the fundamental motives underlying and causing behavior.

So far we have looked at these processes from a biblical perspective, seeking understanding from Scripture. In this chapter we will see an overview of what secular research suggests about the development of conscience and commitment.

Goals

The secular educator is also concerned about commitment. History reveals all too starkly that a determined leadership can shape the thinking and behavior of a generation. Hitler applied such pressures, and the youth of Germany conformed to his standards. A whole culture was warped and twisted. Against history's background, how important it seems to know how to develop a moral man in an immoral world, one who will adopt and act on ethical principles which may run counter to the trend of his society.

Certainly this is the problem of the Christian. We hold to a revealed truth, a whole way of life, and a commitment to love that runs against the grain of a society of men—men who, being of the world and under the sway of sin and Satan build their lives on different values. Can the Christian live in this world, and yet live as citizen of another country? Can the believer behave as a member of God's family, while in a pagan society? We have to answer yes to these questions. But we also have to realize that all sorts of pressures act on the believer to shape his way of thinking and feeling to the ways of the world. If any parent needs to understand how to develop commitment to principles *not* expressed in the general society, it is the Christian parent.

And so the goal set by the secular researcher is in fullest harmony with the goal set by the Christian. Both seek to develop independent personalities, persons who will act on inner values which are a part of their very character. We want no man or woman who when in Rome will do as the Romans do. We want to bring up no young people who, when in college, will adopt the morals and values of much of their college community.

How character develops

Peck and Havighurst, in an older book, suggest a framework for understanding character development that later research enriches and expands.* Basically, the processes suggested are these:

Reward and punishment. As a young child grows, he quickly becomes aware of the desires of those around him, especially those of his parents. We communicate approval and disapproval in many ways. Our child does something that pleases us. We smile and nod our head, or reach out to give him a warm hug, or say, in a happy voice, "Good boy!" In these simple ways of showing approval we reward him, for our approval is intensely important to one whose early world is his mother and father.

In the same way, a child quickly becomes aware of our disapproval. He sees the look on our face. He senses our withdrawal from him. He feels a barrier that cuts off the flow of warmth.

This kind of reward and punishment is what Havighurst has primarily in mind. The explicit reward ("Here's candy for being such a good boy") and the explicit punishment

*Robert F. Peck and Robert J. Havighurst, *The Psychology of Character Development* (New York: Wiley, 1960).

("I'm going to have to spank you") are a part, but not a vital part, of reward-and-punishment communication.

We can begin to see here why it is so important for parents to hold clear-cut values of their own. Fairchild and Wynn, in their book on families, point out that a key problem in nominally Christian homes is parental indecision on their own standards and values!† When Mom and Dad are uncertain about their own values, they have no consistent way of life to communicate. Their reactions to their children, their instinctive approval and disapproval, will communicate only their own uncertainty and confusion. It is when parents have worked through their own values that Mom and Dad will communicate a pattern of life from the child's earliest days that testifies to the biblical values that underlie it.

Jay and his wife were considering buying a new rug. They had talked about it at the dinner table for several weeks. Should they buy one now? How much should they spend? What other things might they need more? Suddenly they realized that in all their talking, they never even thought to pray about this major purchase, or to ask God's guidance.

What impact had their weeks of talk had on their children? What impression had the children developed of the decision-making process? What values had been communicated?

When Christian parents seek to link their lives to the Lord, and respond to their children and to the situations that arise in life from the core of their own commitment to God's ways, then, through the simple process of "reward and punishment" foundations of character are being laid.

Unconscious imitation. Later researchers have learned more about the processes through which what Havighurst called "unconscious imitation" takes place. And there is still general agreement that as a child grows, he begins, unconsciously, to imitate those who are important to him.

†Roy W. Fairchild and John C. Wynn, *Families in the Church* (New York: Association Press, 1961).

A study of Wheaton College students performed as doctoral research by a professor there shows how great the impact of unconscious imitation is. He studied freshmen's preceptions of themselves and others. Each participant rated himself and several other persons (such as a parent, or a teacher) for a variety of personality traits (such as warm, cold, intelligent, slow). The results showed that most freshmen saw themselves as strikingly like the parent they chose to analyze. If Dad was viewed as a warm person, the collegian tended to see himself as warm too—to almost the same degree!

There was no conscious attempt here to be like Mom or Dad. Somehow the growing young person simply pictures himself as being like his parent. And he acts out of that self-image.

We can see even more how vital it is that our lives express the reality of God and His Word, and why Jay and his wife were upset when they realized that they had not been linking something that was really important to them to the Lord. If his children really imitate Jay, how will they behave when *they* have an important decision to make?

Unconscious imitation also involves the formation, as a child grows older, of an "idealized self." A picture of the person he would like to be.

We have all seen this in teens. A guy studies the moves of a sports star, and practices them in the backyard, dreaming of the day when he will be out there on the playing field doing the deeds of his hero. A girl tries out the hairdo of a favorite model or TV personality. These young people are trying to form a picture of their idealized self—of the person they hope they are going to become—and are testing behaviors that fit their image.

How important that we as parents give them a model of a Christian here, that they might see Jesus Christ in us, and look to Him as their ideal.

Reflective thinking. This last process suggested by Peck and

Havighurst has in it the dimension of conscious choice. The
other processes will operate in daily living, without the awareness of either parent or child. But there comes a time when a
young person is very much aware of different values and different ways of life than those he has seen in his home. There
come times of decision, times when he will look ahead and
decide "This is what I will do. This is the kind of person I
choose to be."

It is at this point that the Christian sees the possibility of
mature commitment to God, a time when our children will
freely choose for themselves the life Christ invites them to
share in Him. When does this time come? This time of mature
choice and reflection? Peck and Havighurst note that in most
young people the capacity to apply moral principles to daily
decisions is quite undeveloped at 16! This does not mean that
mature commitment can't take place in, and be expressed during, the teenage years. But it is a distinct possibility that the
time of commitment for most young people comes during the
college years, when they have left the home, and suddenly
found that they *must* choose.

Throughout our time with our children, then, we need to
be working toward the days of commitment. We have to
realize that a time will come when each of our children will
be on his own, free to choose God's way—or some other
way. Which way will he choose? Is there anything we can do
to facilitate the free choice Christ's way?

Personality types

In their study, Peck and Havighurst suggested four types of
personality. These types are classified by moral character—
by their response to moral principles and values. Then Peck
and Havighurst went on to suggest the parent behaviors that
are most likely to produce each type.

One personality type they label *expedient*. This person fits
in whatever the pattern of values around him. Is he at church?

Then he will appear pious, do what is expected, and perhaps even share a warm testimony if this is the "thing to do" in his fellowship. Is he at school? If he is with one crowd, he will squat in the back hall with the guys and smoke grass. He will fit in wherever he is. He will do as others around him do.

What kind of parents did he have? Probably parents who supported and accepted him, but who did not demand obedience or love. Parents who gave him no clear-cut pattern of right and wrong, and who, in general, left him alone to go his own way.

Another personality type is labeled *amoral*. This is the angry, rebellious person, who strikes out and who acts on his impulses and instincts without regard for moral principles or the rights of others. Peck and Havighurst say he is typically a rejected child, one who in his own home has known distrust, inconsistence, rejection, and harsh discipline.

A third type is that of the *conformer*. On the surface he appears to be the ideal child or youth. Even as an adult he is likely to continue to do the right thing. But his behavior does not spring from love and a desire to respond—those motives the Bible presents as so vital in Christian experience. As an adult, this person is likely to realize suddenly that his faith and his life are empty, and in despair will wonder if there is any meaning in all that he has been taught and has thought he believed.

What factors tend to produce a conforming personality? The key seems to be that his parents are consistent authoritarians. They provide regularity and rules and standards: they also trust him and give him approval. But with all this, there is autocratic control and severe discipline—a lack of freedom to learn to make his own choices, and immediate punishment for straying from a prescribed path.

The fourth personality type suggested is the *rational-altruistic.*, who, Havighurst says, is marked by well-integrated, mature, internalized moral principles, on which he acts, rather than acting on "rules." This person usually has felt a sense of participation in his parents' lives, and has had consistent example and expectation from them. They have let him make decisions, helped to explain reasons, given him trust and approval, and have been consistent (and lenient) in discipline.

Peck and Havighurst's four personality types and their causes could be broken down into the chart on page 109.

There have been many later studies of the development of conscience in children. Over and over again, conclusions have been similar to those of Peck and Havighurst. The way we bring up our children does have a definite impact on their character, and on the kind of persons they become. We must realize that the way we nurture our boys and girls will have a great and a God-intended impact on their Christian experience.

Principles reviewed

If we were to summarize guidelines for child nurture one gleans from researchers, we might well come up with a list like this.

Incentive. Incentive for ethical behavior is provided by the bonds of life. We cannot *make* a person choose the right way. But we can draw him by love toward God and His ways. A climate of love in the home and expression of love for the child remains crucial.

Guidance. The child needs adult guidance at each stage of his development. When he is young, firm and clear direction is important. As he grows older, guidance that is appropriate to his stage of life is still required.

Example patterns. No single experience shapes the personality. The example provided by adults, as a whole pattern of life lived out before the child, is important. How vital that we live God's way, and that our life model the words of our God.

What the child is like	What the parents are like	What the home is like
Expedient	Supportive without demanding obedience or love	No clear right-wrong pattern Laissez-faire atmosphere
Amoral	Rejective of the child	Distrust Inconsistence Rejection Harsh discipline
Conformer	Consistently authoritarian	Regularity, rules Trust and approval Autocratic control Severe discipline
Rational-Altruistic	Well-integrated, mature Internalized moral principles acted on rather than rules	Consistence Mutual participation Shared decisions Trust and approval Consistent, lenient discipline

Trust and approval. When parents trust their children and show approval, the children are most likely to grow into healthy and free persons. Praise is a more important part of raising children than punishment: communicating one's approval is a vital part of encouraging response to God.

Consistent discipline. Again, consistent and lenient discipline is stressed. Punishment does play a part in guiding our children: but harsh punishment or harsh methods of obtaining obedience are ultimately self-defeating. And, where love is present, such methods are unnecessary.

Mutual participation. Growth is facilitated when the child is involved, and when parents and children talk things over. Explanation of actions and of requests is important.

Making decisions. As a child grows, he should be encouraged to begin making his own choices. More and more responsibility can be extended as he shows greater ability to make decisions wisely.

Summarizing, we might say that from the point of view of research, the best homes are those in which children are given reasons to feel incentives (love, approval), and where parents guide their children intelligently, giving growing freedom for them to make their own decisions. No other approach will bring us beyond compliance: no other will encourage commitment.

REACT

1. Why do you think there is apparent harmony between biblical and secular principles for developing mature persons through the home?
2. How would you answer an objection to these approaches based on the notion that Christians must depend only on supernatural means for encouraging their children to respond to Christ?

ACT

1. Look through the chapter again. Particularly see if you can determine what kind of personalities your present practices are most likely to produce.

10
Christon Within

At the beginning of this book, we got a
glimpse of God's great goal for us and for our
children. We saw that it involved coming to
love the Lord, and, with love motivating us, to
respond to Him in willing obedience.

But Scripture contains an even more vivid
statement of God's goal. We hear it in
Christ's words: "You are to be perfect, as your
heavenly Father" (Mt 5:48).

Rich Little is an imitator. He can twist his voice to mimic the voices of well-known people. While still himself, he can sound like someone else.

The Christian is not to be this kind of imitator. Christ did not invite His disciples to embark on a life of hypocrisy, pretending to act and feel like God. Jesus said we are to *be* like, not *act* like, our heavenly Father.

The New Testament continually reflects this goal. We believers have been called by God "to bear the family likeness of his Son, that he might be the eldest of a family of many brothers" (Ro 8:29, Phillips). And Peter commands, "Don't let your character be molded by the desires of your ignorant days, but be holy in every department of your lives, for the one who has called you is himself holy. The Scripture says: Ye shall be holy; for I am holy" (1 Pe 1:14-15, Phillips). *We are to be like our heavenly Father.*

But how can this be? Peter goes on to point out to believers that in responding to the truth of the gospel, "You have . . . made your souls clean enough for a genuine love of your fellows. . . . For you are sons of God now; the live, permanent Word of the living God has given you his own indestructible heredity" (1 Pe 1:22-23, Phillips). We can be like God, for when we trust Christ as Saviour, God plants His nature deep within our personalities; we become His sons and share His heredity.

Thus all of life for you and me becomes a growing process. Having been born again, and in new birth launched on an adventure through time and eternity, we are destined to ever know more and more of God, and to grow more and more like Him. So Paul labors over his converts "until Christ be formed in you" (Gal 4:19, KJV), and yearns for the day "when we all attain to the unity of the faith, and of the knowledge of the Son of God to mature man, to the measure of the stature which belongs to the fullness of Christ." For in every way, "We are to grow up in all aspects into Him, who is the head, even Christ" (Eph 4:13-15).

It is this that is at the heart of our faith: this that is "the riches of the glory of this mystery . . . which is Christ in you, the hope of glory" (Col 1:27).

Someone has said, "Christianity is Christ." It is even more true to say, "Christianity is Christ *within!*"

Seeing our faith in this light, as God's own life planted in human hearts and growing there until the individual personality is transformed to bear the stamp of the Father, helps us to understand better the nature of Christian nurture and the importance of the home.

Implications for Christian nurture

Conversion. One of the first implications for us is clear. Before a person can grow in God's likeness, he must own God's heredity. He must be born again, and by faith in Jesus have become a son of the Father (cf. Gal 3:26).

We can never look at Christian nurture as a purely natural process through which human nature is guided to reflect some "spark of the divine" within. As parents, we need to recognize the fact that our children, whom we love and whom we value for themselves, are yet sinners who will need to know God's forgiveness and receive new life from His hand. So seeing our children respond to the good news and to the redeeming love of Jesus is one of our greatest desires—and greatest privileges.

Much has been written about conversion of children, and about leading your child to Christ. Too often in such approaches, "faith" has been equated with a verbal transaction—with getting your child to say the Bible words or to "invite Christ into his heart."

How real are such childhood "conversions"? I have no doubt that some are very real, that faith can be awakened in the youngest of hearts. But I also have no doubt that many such conversions are simply responses made to please Mom or Dad or teacher, something done because a loved adult seems to expect and want it. We need not hesitate to share in simple words the truth that Jesus loves and died for our boy or girl. But we should not place great emphasis on an early verbal response or acceptance of the gospel. As Jesus said, "The wind blows where it likes, you can hear the sound of it but you have no idea where it comes from and where it goes. Nor can you tell how a man is born by the wind of the Spirit" (Jn 3:8, Phillips). God works in hearts His way, in His time, by His will.

What does his mean for us parents? First, that we need to look to God in prayer to bring our children to Him. God loves us and He loves our child: this we know, and this gives us confidence as we ask Him to work in our children's lives.

Second, we need to share God's Word and ways with our children as they grow, so that from their earliest memories, they sense the reality of Jesus' love in our love for them. Through what we do and say, the growing child can be aware that God is present in his home as One to whom we turn together in prayer and thanksgiving. One whom we love to please.

Third, we can teach, telling our children more and more of Jesus as they grow, answering the questions that arise, ready always to help them understand that this Jesus, whose love they have always known, is also Saviour. We can be ready, when God is ready and our children are ready, to support awakening faith.

Fourth, we can realize that conversion is always a beginning, never an end. Before and after Christ enters the personality, a child will need the same kind of guidance and teaching. For as a child grows through the various stages of life, his ability to understand and to respond will grow too, and he needs a consistent example from his parents to drink in all that God would teach him.

When new life comes, we have a fresh beginning. Through love and gentleness, both the birth and the growth are encouraged.

Growth. When we see Christian faith as the constant growth of life God plants in us at conversion, we realize that childhood is not the only growing time. And so we have to view our task as parents as launching our children on a lifetime of growth. Children need to learn from their years with us how to live in obedience to the Word of God, thus expressing and experiencing the love of God (Jn 14:23-24). And they need to learn the context of openness and love in which growth can best take place.

Learning how to love and be loved is of vital importance. Because the growing years extend throughout our lives, you and I, as well as our children, will have a continuing need for growth in Christ. And God has provided for our need!

How? In the church, as an extended family of men and women who come together around Jesus Christ, to worship Him and to help each other grow. In the New Testament, the church is not a building or even a congregation. The church is a fellowship of saints, a great family in which each of us can encourage and build up the other in our Christian lives. The same context of love that provides the climate for growth in the home is to mark the church! Every passage in this book quoted about the climate of growth has direct application in the Scriptures to the way Christians are to live together as God's greater family!

When we teach our children to love and to be loved, to forgive and accept forgiveness, to seek reconciliation and value unity, to live together in openness and honesty, then they may take these essential qualities with them into the fellowship of believers when they become adults. If so, the future of Christ's church on earth will be brighter than in our present experience!

What we do in our homes touches not only the lives of our

own boys and girls; it affects the whole work of God in the world of tomorrow.

"Belief" inadequate. Christian faith is Christ within, growing more and more to fill our lives with His love and character. When we see our faith this way, we realize how inadequate it is to think of Christian nurture as the communication of beliefs alone.

Much of our effort in the church today is focused merely on the transmission of beliefs. We teach as though all that were necessary is for a young person to know certain things about the Bible and to accept them. We preach God's Word from our pulpits, but seem to expect little more from most who find places in our pews than financial support for our programs, and an orthodoxy of belief that will permit us to take pride in our "true to the Bible" stand. Yet if we are really true to the Bible, we can be satisfied with nothing less than *growing* Christians, persons whose lives are marked out by Christlikeness and love.

And so we turn again to the importance of the home in Christian nurture. In the few briew hours in the church and its agencies each week, little more can be done than to talk about what it is we believe. The full content of faith—the attitudes and feelings and actions that are in harmony with our beliefs—these are learned from persons who provide examples of Christlike life, persons whom the learners come to know intimately and to love well. The first example, the most powerful model for a child, is you, the parent.

This is no attack on church or Sunday school. This is simply a recognition of the fact that the church and its agencies can not do the job of Christian nurture. Only the home, only you, can provide the fullest and most compelling training in faith. "You shall teach them diligently to your children" are words of command that God has never withdrawn. They are words rooted, as is every divine command, in the nature of things. Only you *can* bring your children toward the fullness of Christian life.

Role of the home. The home, then, has the unique role in Christian nurture. The home is the place where, from his earliest days, a child sees orthodox belief enfleshed with all the attitudes and feelings and love that grow when Christ infuses the believer and transforms his life.

When a climate of love exists in which communication can take place, when we as parents have God's words rooted deeply in our hearts and expressed naturally in our lives, and when we link our actions verbally to the words of God from which they spring—then our children will grow up with true faith. This true faith knows Christ, not as someone about whom certain things are true and to be believed, but as a living reality within.

Church and Sunday school

I know that some must view me as an enemy of church and Sunday school. They will probably take much in this book as an attack on these institutions. For this I am sorry, for I see myself as a friend.

What I am an enemy of, driven to this position by the Word that we all study as our standard and guide, is the failure to recognize or unwillingness to admit the limitations of our current approaches in Christian education.

At its best, the Sunday school can *never* replace or perform the ministry of the home. Our failure to admit this, and to seek ways to strengthen the home and link it with Sunday school in a cooperative system, is something that we need to face. One great task of the church today, as renewal gives impetus to rethinking the nature and purpose of the local church, is to find ways to shift the center of nurture back into the home, to help parents fulfill their ministry rather than implying, by ignoring the home, that the local church and its agencies are adequate to bring up children in the fear and admonition of the Lord.

What, then, can we do? Here are three things that we can do right now. There are others that await the future.

First, parents can work with the present Sunday school programs. Remember that the unique contribution of the home is to make *real* (through living example) the truths taught in the words of Scripture. Thus when we parents know what is being taught at church, we can seek ways to integrate and express the same truths in a living way at home.

Yet few parents bother to find out what their children are being taught in Sunday school! If there is to be a translation of truth from information to living reality, parents must care about this kind of cooperation.

Second, teachers can seek to bring life into the classroom. This series of Moody books, the Effective Teaching Series, is designed to help teachers of all age groups discover what can be done to better link Bible truths with the attitudes and feelings and behaviors that are involved in experiencing them. If you are interested in seeing how this can be done, and in principles that parents can apply in teaching at home, see the first book of the series, *You, the Teacher*.

Third, while the two steps noted above can be taken now, they are stopgap measures. Across the years, we've seen many advances in Sunday school curriculum, pioneered by various publishers. In the future we will see additional changes—even more significant ones. Even the best of present curriculums seeks to implement an educational philosophy that is classroom oriented; not a philosophy rooted in the biblical concept of communication of faith-as-life. What we need, and what we will see, is a new kind of Christian education system, which links church and home in such a way as to focus nurture in the home, and to provide parents with the guidance they need to share God's truth in natural, living ways.

And for you?

What does it mean for you, now, to be a Christian parent? Just what we have been speaking of in this book. Now, and most important, it means being a growing Christian yourself. It means building in your home that climate that facilitates communication. It means living God's Word by example.

As you and I become more like our heavenly Father in every way, God the Holy Spirit can and will use us to touch the hearts, and the lives, of our children.

REACT

1. In your own words, state why the author says Sunday school cannot do the job of Christian nurture.
2. State in your own words the unique task of the home in the ministry of nurture.

ACT

1. Check with your children's Sunday school teachers to see what they are studying. See if your Sunday school superintendent, your director of Christian education, or your pastor can help you find ways to coordinate your church and home efforts.
2. Look over the book **You, the Teacher** (Moody Press) for suggestions on how a teacher communicates most effectively. See how the suggestions can be applied in your own home.